Great American Paintings

from the Boston and

Metropolitan Museums

National Gallery of Art

City Art Museum, St. Louis

Seattle Art Museum

Great American Paintings

from the Boston and Metropolitan Museums

by Thomas N. Maytham

Seattle Art Museum

Exhibition Dates:

The National Gallery of Art
Washington, D.C.
November 30, 1970–January 10, 1971

The City Art Museum
St. Louis, Missouri
January 28–March 7, 1971

The Seattle Art Museum
Seattle, Washington
March 25–May 9, 1971

Foreword

This year, the Museum of Fine Arts, Boston and the Metropolitan Museum of Art, New York share the good fortune of celebrating their hundredth anniversaries, marking a century of dedication to collecting, preserving, and interpreting the art of the world for past and future generations. It is especially appropriate that both museums should collaborate in a major venture, one that will enable broad segments of the country to participate directly in the Centennial celebrations. We therefore welcomed the proposal of the Seattle Art Museum to organize an exhibition of masterworks of American painting drawn from our collections, to travel to three major American cities.

The Seattle Art Museum, working with our staffs, has selected one hundred American paintings, ranging in date from 1670 to 1969, which reveal the major stylistic developments in American art. We would like to express sincere appreciation to the Seattle Art Museum for organizing the exhibition and preparing the catalogue. We also offer our thanks to the Trustees and staffs of the National Gallery of Art in Washington, D.C. and the City Art Museum of St. Louis whose museums will share the exhibition. We extend particular thanks to the Department of Paintings at the Boston Museum, to the Departments of American Painting and Sculpture and Contemporary Arts at the Metropolitan Museum, and to many others at both museums who have generously and ably contributed to the realization of this exhibition.

We feel the Centennials of two of the greatest art museums in the western hemisphere are events not just of local but of national significance. Therefore, we are proud that tens of thousands of citizens from throughout the country, as well as visitors from many nations, will have this opportunity to see major works from our collections and thus to find insights into the nature of American life and art.

PERRY TOWNSEND RATHBONE
Director
Museum of Fine Arts, Boston

THOMAS P. F. HOVING
Director
The Metropolitan Museum of Art, New York

Acknowledgements

The exhibition GREAT AMERICAN PAINTINGS from the Boston and Metropolitan Museums has been organized as a national salute to the one-hundredth anniversaries of these museums. Primary among the many goals of the exhibition is to mark the high quality of American painting which is so brilliantly represented in their collections, and to broaden participation in the Centennial event. Exhibitions of American painting date back to the nineteenth century and have flourished in the past several decades. Yet, never before has an exhibition of American painting of comparable quality been drawn from only two collections. Nor have so many of the masterpieces in these renowned collections ever been brought together. The cities of Washington, D.C., St. Louis, and Seattle, while acquainted with American painting, have rarely if ever had the privilege of exposure to an American exhibition of this stature.

As a former member of the Department of Paintings at the Boston Museum, I have long admired the exceptional American painting collections at the Boston and Metropolitan Museums. With the approach of the Centennial Anniversary year, I sought for an appropriate tribute to these two vital institutions in the form of an exhibition that would unite important segments from their collections. Since American painting is one of the major fields in which both museums are unexcelled, it seemed the ideal area for collaboration.

Although the Seattle Art Museum has organized the exhibition, it is abundantly clear that its quality is in full measure the consequence of extraordinary generosity on the part of the Trustees and Staffs of the Boston and Metropolitan Museums. In making selections, quality was the uppermost criterion. Yet, it seemed also important on an anniversary occasion to assess the nature and achievements not of a limited time period but of the entire course of American painting. No absolute standard of quality can be applied throughout and each work therefore must be viewed in the context of the artist and his period. Consequently, exceptional paintings by relatively minor artists appear alongside masterpieces by major figures.

The exhibition is not intended specifically as a survey of American painting. Not even two collections such as these can fully chronicle that complex history within one hundred pictures and still maintain the necessarily high standards of quality. Fortunately, the Boston and Metropolitan collections tend to supplement rather than duplicate each other. The Boston collection is unparalleled in its riches of eighteenth- and early and mid-nineteenth-century painting, particularly from New England. The Metropolitan Museum possesses great masterpieces of virtually all periods, but is especially strong in the mid to later nineteenth century, and in recent years has established a twentieth-century collection of remarkable caliber.

To select one hundred paintings – fifty from each museum – from the treasures available inevitably demands some arbitrary decisions. In addition, either for reasons of size, condition, or commitment to other exhibitions, several highly desirable paintings were unavailable. The final selection is intended, however, to offer major works representative of most of the important periods, movements, and artists which comprise the fabric of American painting.

My profoundest debt of gratitude is to Perry Rathbone and Thomas Hoving, Directors respectively of the Boston and Metropolitan Museums. Without their sympathetic support the exhibition would not exist at all. Their cooperative liberality is matched by the Presidents and Boards of Trustees of their museums who, during the Centennial Year, waived on our behalf their natural desire to have their best works on view at home.

On behalf of the Seattle Art Museum and my colleagues at the National Gallery of Art and the City Art Museum of St. Louis, I would like to extend our deep appreciation for the privilege of presenting these treasures and simultaneously for extending participation in the great centennial event to the nation at large.

In preparation of the exhibition and its catalogue, I have incurred numerous debts for assistance and advice. At the Metropolitan Museum I offer my appreciation to George Trescher, Secretary of the 100th Anniversary Committee, and his staff for their consistent enthusiasm and helpfulness. Particular thanks are due John K. Howat, Associate Curator of American Paintings and Sculpture, and his Assistant, Miss Natalie Spassky, for their aid in making selections and providing extensive catalogue information; to Henry Geldzahler, Curator of the Department of Contemporary Arts, and his Assistant Curator, James Wood; to Theodore Rousseau, Vice-Director; to William Wilkinson, Registrar, and to Leon Wilson, Editor of Publications.

At the Boston Museum I am indebted to Diggory Venn, Special Assistant to the Director, for his enthusiastic support of the project; to Miss Laura Luckey and Mrs. Lucretia Giese, my former associates in the Department of Paintings; to Mrs. Susan Oakie Bush, former Registrar and Miss Patricia Alward, Editor of Publications. All have given generously of their time and efforts. I am especially grateful to Carl F. Zahn, for his design of the catalogue and to my friend, Mrs. Jean G. Crocker of New York who has selflessly and skillfully edited the catalogue.

I am also grateful to the Editorial and Curatorial staffs at both lending museums for their generous permission to consult and liberally utilize both published and manuscript catalogue information. Those sources are the product of many people's efforts but special recognition should be made of the work of Mrs. Haven Parker and Mrs. Arianwen Howard Neve, formerly of the Boston Museum; the late Albert T. E. Gardner and Stuart Feld, formerly of the Metropolitan Museum; and to John Howat and Henry Geldzahler. Their research and writings have been immensely valuable to me.

I owe special thanks to J. Carter Brown, Director of the National Gallery, William P. Campbell, Assistant Chief Curator there and Charles Buckley, Director of the City Art Museum of St. Louis for their active participation in the exhibition. Above all, I owe my fullest appreciation to Dr. Richard E. Fuller, President and Director of the Seattle Art Museum, who has patiently endured the vicissitudes of the project, and sustained his firm support of it.

An exhibition of this caliber and dimension makes unusual financial demands. With pride and appreciation I thank the Washington State Arts Commission for its substantial subsidy to the Seattle Art Museum. Their generosity has helped make possible a major event in the cultural life of this region.

On the staff of the Seattle Art Museum I am particularly grateful to Mrs. Myrna Torrie for her faithful dedication to the monumental tasks of correspondence and catalogue preparation; to Mrs. Sue Kent for preparing the Bibliography, and to Mrs. Coe V. Malone, Mrs. Jill Armstrong and Miss Hermie Lyons for ready assistance in a variety of ways.

THOMAS N. MAYTHAM
Associate Director
Seattle Art Museum

Introduction

by Thomas N. Maytham

In the course of three centuries, American painting has developed from earnest attempts by early portrait limners through a burgeoning florescence in the eighteenth and nineteenth centuries to a position of international leadership in modern times. From the beginning, the majority of American artists looked to Europe for inspiration, and even in recent decades European emigrants have exerted important influences on the nature and direction of American painting. Yet, since the early eighteenth century, all forms of art in America and especially painting, have displayed a distinctly American accent. American painters, craftsmen in furniture, silver and pewter, and architects, have metamorphosed contemporaneous European styles into an identifiable and consistently American form.

Throughout the centuries, Americans have treasured works of art as permanent records of their personal lives and new land, and later as examples of a growing aesthetic identity. Today, thousands of paintings, and countless other works in every medium, constitute a major part of the cultural and historical patrimony of our nation.

Since the early nineteenth century, much of the finest of American arts have gravitated from the parlors and attics of American homes to the museums which have become the public custodians and interpreters of our artistic heritage. There they offer a detailed panorama of the course of American life and the vision of our artists.

Through the end of the nineteenth century, Boston, New York and Philadelphia were the foremost centers of cultural life in America. Predictably they were among the earliest to establish cultural institutions, and American art and artists were part of the generative force. Charles Willson Peale, the Philadelphia painter and patriarch of the clan of important artists, founded his own museum late in the eighteenth century as well as the Columbianum, antecedent of the Pennsylvania Academy of the Fine Arts. The Boston Athenaeum, parent of the Museum of Fine Arts, began to offer annual exhibitions and to acquire American painting in 1827. Similarly, several important painters were active in the formation of the Metropolitan Museum in 1870 and were founding members of its Board.

Combinations of circumstances have helped to sustain the Boston and Metropolitan Museums in the front rank. While artists were directly or indirectly involved with their creation, socially concerned leaders of the financial and intellectual communities provided the major impetus. The economic, political and social upheaval of the Civil War had shaken the somewhat idyllic complacency of American society. Leaders of late Victorian society became deeply conscious of the cultural status of the nation. Aware of the rich treasure houses of Europe in Florence, Rome and Paris, they believed it imperative that our maturing nation must establish similar cultural resources. Prompted both by national pride and moral responsibility, they initiated discussions which rapidly led to concrete proposals for permanent public collections.

In Boston, prominent citizens, including John Amory Lowell, President of the

Boston Athenaeum, conceived of a museum which could build upon the already large collections held by the Athenaeum, Harvard University and the recently formed Massachusetts Institute of Technology. After incorporation of the museum by the Massachusetts legislature in February of 1870, a committee to solicit public funds soon amassed a quarter of a million dollars and on July 4, 1876, the first brick and terracotta structure in Copley Square opened to the public. The first acquisition was prophetic. It was not only a painting, but by an American artist and of masterful quality, the *Elijah in the Desert* (cat. no. 26) by the adopted favorite, Washington Allston, given by Mrs. Samuel Hooper and Miss Alice Hooper in 1870.

Simultaneously, New Yorkers were agitating for a museum of art. In the 1860's influential citizens, artists and authors, expressed their desire for a "free Gallery of Art in our cities" as the historian Tuckerman phrased it, "a benign provision for and promotion of high civilization," intended for the advancement of public taste. The prestigious and exclusive Union League Club was the cradle for the project. Publisher George P. Putman was chairman of the Club's Art Committee whose members included artists John Kensett and Worthington Whittredge, and the collector and patron, Samuel P. Avery. In November of 1869, William Cullen Bryant himself addressed a meeting to establish the Museum of Art, and in due course, the Metropolitan Museum of Art was incorporated in April of the following year. Kensett's bequest of a large number of his paintings in 1872 was the first important step towards the present exceptional American collection.

While the course of American painting can be followed, even in detail, in either the Boston or Metropolitan collection, if combined they tend to supplement rather than duplicate each other. Of greatest importance, as can be seen in this selection, is the abundance of masterworks. Each testifies to an individual genius, and in concert they form an articulate expression of the creative spirit of our nation.

Little remains to visually document the nature of life in the first century of habitation of the continent. A scant two dozen paintings have survived from the seventeenth century, many of little more than antiquarian interest. One of the finest among them however is the portrait of *Robert Gibbs* (cat. no. 1), painted exactly three centuries ago. While the artist is unknown, this and other identifiable works by the same hand link American painting with earlier traditions of European secular painting. As such it stands at one pole in American art. Its sources lie not in contemporary English or Netherlandish painting, already in a Baroque phase, but in the decoratively detailed late medieval style which persisted in provincial areas well into the seventeenth century. Despite stiffness its elaborate stylization enhances the intrinsic charm of the subject.

Portraits remained the dominant and in fact almost exclusive concern of American painters – and their patrons – through the early nineteenth century. Waning of the Puritan ethic in the early eighteenth century and the growth of an increasingly rich and stable economy allowed emulation of the luxury of European society. Portraits of religious leaders were replaced by a rapidly growing demand for likenesses of the leading merchants and their ladies. While a few craftsmen executed portrait commissions in the early eighteenth century, the first important artists to settle in America were Peter Pelham and John Smibert, who arrived from England in 1727 and 1729, respectively. Both were professionally trained in the rather ponderous Baroque style of Sir Godfrey Kneller, the German painter who dominated court art in early eighteenth century England. Smibert established a studio and art supply shop in Boston, married well and produced during the next twenty years numbers of portraits of the merchant elite and their families. His robust portraits of *Mr. and Mrs. Francis Brinley* (cat. nos. 2, 3) are among the finest of his early work.

John Singleton Copley was the first to significantly alter the course established by Smibert, and to provide the nation with its first great master. As stepson of Peter Pelham, Copley was raised in an artistic milieu, absorbing both Pelham's and Smibert's style. Proficient at fifteen, he surpassed all his colleagues by twenty and remained the leading artist in America until departure for England in 1774. Robert Feke of Long Island and the English artist Joseph Blackburn were the most significant of his contemporaries. The enigmatic Feke developed a more sophisticated version of Smibert's Baroque, as seen in his skillful portrait of the young Boston merchant *Isaac Winslow* (cat. no. 5).

In the 1750's, Joseph Blackburn, trained in England, introduced the delicate and colorful Rococo style fashionable in mid-century London. His superlative group portrait of the same *Isaac Winslow and His Family* (cat. no. 4) typifies the example which he set for young Copley. Copley's attention to Blackburn's lessons soon appeared in such masterful works as the brilliant double portrait of *Mary and Elizabeth Royall* (cat. no. 7) of 1758, one of America's earliest masterpieces. During the next fifteen years, Copley developed an increasingly refined yet inventive style. His elegant portrait of the lovely *Mrs. Richard Skinner* (cat. no.10), his sure characterization of the casual yet alertly intelligent *Nicholas Boylston* (cat. no. 8), and the radically informal portrayal of his fellow craftsman, *Paul Revere* (cat. no. 9), are all aspects of his individuality.

Copley's dramatic subject piece, *Watson and the Shark* (cat. no. 11), is a major monument of his career. Painted but two years after his arrival in London, its realistic depiction in the grand manner of an ordinary event substantially developed the ideas of Benjamin West, and still anticipated by forty years the celebrated innovations of the French Romantic painters. The greater part of Copley's long career was spent in England, where he adapted to the freer and more flattering portrait manner. A measure of his success is his famous portrait of *Midshipman Brine* (cat. no.12).

Charles Willson Peale and the Connecticut artists Ralph Earl and John Trumbull all had admired Copley's painting in America, and had worked with the expatriate West in his London studio. Peale and Earl in different ways continued the colonial portrait tradition through the end of the eighteenth century. Influenced also by Reynolds, Peale's portraits, such as that of *Mrs. Mifflin and her Granddaughter* (cat.

no.13) were more gracious and urbane than the powerful and often colorful work of Earl. Trumbull was influenced less by West's and Copley's style than their success with monumental battle and historical painting, which was the inspiration for his lifelong dedication to immortalizing the heroes and events of the American Revolution.

In *The American School* (cat. no.18) Matthew Pratt skillfully documented the pivotal function of Benjamin West: the open-hearted, genial teacher. West's remarkable talents and character had transported him from rural Pennsylvania to the immensely influential position of Historical Painter of the King of England and President of the Royal Academy. Despite his significant contributions to establishment of the Neoclassical style in England, his impact as an artist was far less important than his assistance of young American artists, who included most of the major painters of the period.

One of the foremost of West's pupils was Gilbert Stuart, later the leading Federal portrait painter. The gifted and mercurial Stuart rapidly earned prominence as a London portraitist, although less influenced by West's art than by the sophisticated styles of Reynolds and Romney. On returning to America, he was soon busily taking likenesses of the financial, political and social leaders of the new nation. His portrait of *Matthew Clarkson* (cat. no. 20), painted in New York soon after his return, reveals the strength and suavity of his English manner. His life portraits of the already legendary *George Washington*, (cat. no. 21), and the scores of replicas after them, confirmed his success. Settled in Boston after 1805, his mature work, such as the brilliant portrait of *Bishop de Cheverus* (cat. no. 22), reveals a sensitive fluency of style and perception of character.

The nineteenth century brought a rapid evolution and maturation of American arts. Although the traditions of the previous century persisted in Federal painting, a succession of movements, largely introduced from Europe, absorbed artists and the public. Neoclassicism, Romanticism and Impressionism each guided the essential American involvement with naturalism into a new channel. Early in the century a spirit of ambitious optimism prevailed. A new sense of national identity, exploration of the wondrous lands to the West, an expanding economy and broader contacts with Europe all encouraged experimentation. Neoclassicism reached America through the work of John Vanderlyn, trained in Paris, and through West's pupil, Thomas Sully of Philadelphia. The earliest major Romantic painter was Washington Allston, much of whose career was spent in England and Rome. Allston was the first to break with convention and to assert the imaginative individuality of the artist. His moody and nostalgic visions of landscape and literary subjects were enthusiastically received in America, particularly in Boston. Among his finest works are the harshly dramatic *Elijah in the Desert* (cat. no. 26), conceived as a religious allegory and once coveted by James Fenimore Cooper, and the idyllic *Moonlit Landscape* (cat. no. 25), painted the next year in 1819. In portraiture, Samuel F. B. Morse's grand and idealizing painting of his daughter as *The Muse* (cat. no. 34), mixed Neoclassic form with Romantic spirit and anticipated the Victorian age.

In the 1820's, landscape painting was established as an independent motif and dominated the second and third quarters of the century. Romanticists discovered in the unspoiled beauty of nature, and its implied reflection of divinity, the purest manifestation of the sublime. In the face of civilization's advance scores of artists sought their inspiration in nature, representing especially its dramatically awesome or sylvan aspects. Robert Salmon, Thomas Birch and Alvan Fisher all had painted landscape in the early part of the century, but Thomas Doughty of Philadelphia and primarily Thomas Cole were the founders of the Romantic tradition of the Hudson River school of landscape painting. Cole, certainly the greatest artist of the school, often turned to religious or allegorical subjects as vehicles for his sentiments on the relationship of nature and man. His magnificent early *Expulsion from the Garden of Eden* (cat. no. 32) is a powerful evocation of the divine splendor of nature and man's relative insignificance. Cole and his numerous followers, including Asher B. Durand, Jasper Francis Cropsey and Frederick Church, established the first essentially American school of painting, Romantic in spirit but committed to naturalism. Church, Cole's pupil, expanded the dramatic element in magnificent visions of burning sunsets and cloudswept mountains and gorges. Cropsey's early work also reveals the influence of Cole, but later his mature painting became more placid and contained. Domesticated panoramas, such as his *Mt. Chocorua, New Hampshire, Autumn* (cat. no. 37) offered assurance of peace and harmony. Durand, originally an important engraver, eulogized the more sylvan aspects of nature, as in his masterwork, *In the Woods* (cat. no. 35).

The second generation of Hudson River artists sought increasingly pictorial goals. Sometimes called Luminists, they emphasized the effects of light and atmoshere in the transient moods of nature. *Kauterskill Falls* (cat. no. 39) by Sanford Gifford, for example, is an immense vista flooded with sun in which colors glow and flicker through soft veils of mist. John Frederick Kensett's masterwork, *Lake George* (cat. no. 38) is a more subtly poetic evocation of silent grandeur, in which the textured slopes of forested mountains tower over a quiet lake.

Fitz Hugh Lane and Martin Johnson Heade are allied members of the group whose names are often linked. Each discovered individual solutions to a common interest in coastal landscape. Lane, whose love of New England's harbors and shoreline is apparent in his view of *Boston Harbor* (cat. no. 43), developed a crisp yet luminously atmospheric style usually phrased in cool, rich color. Heade's famous *Approaching Storm: Beach Near Newport* (cat. no. 47), like so many of his works, vividly captures the changing moods of nature, here the sharp light and looming threat of a passing coastal storm. Both artists are among many that were effectively recovered from oblivion by the Boston patron, Maxim Karolik, whose collection contains thirteen works by Lane and twenty-nine by Heade.

An important tradition of naive or primitive painting persisted from the seventeenth century and flourished in the nineteenth. As an increasing population settled rural regions, a growing demand arose for portraits, landscape and decorative painting. Until the general advent of photography, great numbers of untrained but able itinerant artists rambled the countryside occasionally producing works of masterful quality. The remarkable *Lady with Her Pets* (cat. no. 15) painted by Rufus Hathaway in the 1790's and the ingenuous and charming *The Falls of Niagara* (cat. no.16) by the Quaker artist Edward Hicks are exceptional examples of early primitive painting. In the mid-nineteenth century, Erastus Salisbury Field's monumental group portrait of *Joseph Moore and His Family* (cat. no. 40) and the diminutive *Meditation by the Sea* (cat. no. 41) by an unknown artist about 1860 reveal the decorative strength and aesthetic sensitivity of which naive painters were capable.

Genre was still another of the prolific motifs to develop in the nineteenth century. Henry Sargent's charming and historically fascinating *The Dinner Party* (cat. no. 27) of about 1820–25 is perhaps the earliest important example. As the century advanced, scores of artists, including Quidor, Thompson, Fisher, and Inman recorded America's pastimes. The instant and universal popularity of genre was spread also through the thousands of engravings offered by the American Art-Union. At mid-century, William Sidney Mount of New York and George Caleb Bingham of the Missouri frontier were the finest in the field. Mount's delightful *Cider Making* (cat. no. 45) reveals the uncontrived style and masterful technique of his best work. Later in the century, Eastman Johnson's arresting and incisive glimpses of rural New Englanders in characteristic moments penetrated the surface of their personalities and infused genre painting with a more profound significance.

The Realist tradition reached its highest point in the painting of Winslow Homer and Thomas Eakins. Homer's earlier paintings were devoted to the casual pleasures of children and young people in the out-of-doors. Among his finest are *Long Branch, New Jersey* (cat. no. 56), so similar to his Impressionist contemporary Boudin, and *Snap the Whip* (cat. no. 54) which capture freshness and movement yet maintain a sense of clarity and detachment. Nature was paramount for Homer, yet his later works became more monumental and isolated in mood, focussing on the drama of man's eternal contest with the sea and the elements.

Where Homer was concerned with the relationship of man and nature, Eakins was committed to discovering the nature of men. His solemnly penetrating portraits of his fellow Philadelphians, especially of professional people, are at once perceptively personal and unflatteringly objective. Even his superb sporting pictures such as *Max Schmitt in a Single Scull* (cat. no. 58) or *Starting Out After Rail* (cat. no. 59) display his disciplined control of composition, color and light creating a unique combination of intensity and reserve.

Trompe l'oeil painting was a popular form of Realist art near the end of the century, with William Harnett and John Frederick Peto the two foremost figures. Harnett's vividly colored *Artist's Card Rack* (cat. no. 62) and monumental late work, *Old Models* (cat. no. 61) are two of his outstanding paintings. The bright charm of

The Poor Man's Store (cat. no. 63) by Peto is an exceptional example of his more informal and richly textured style.

Contemporaneous with the Realist giants, Homer and Eakins, two major figures of the Romantic tradition, Ralph Blakelock and Albert Pinkham Ryder, worked virtually unnoticed. Inventing intensely personal styles, they created remote, melancholy worlds of idealized fantasy or romantic tragedy. The *Indian Encampment* (cat. no. 65) by Blakelock is a beautiful and characteristic example of his moody and mysterious woodland scenes. Ryder's art, as in his painting, *Constance* (cat. no. 66), is rich in the emotional and theatrical spirit of his sources in Romantic literature and legend.

After the Civil War, American artists traveled to Europe for study in increasing numbers. Some such as Inness, Hunt and Babcock worked at Barbizon, others entered the fashionable academies of Paris, Munich and Düsseldorf, or worked under individual masters. Three major painters, Sargent, Whistler and Cassatt, made Europe their home. John Singer Sargent, born in Europe of American parents, was a precocious genius destined to become a leading portraitist in fashionable circles of Paris, London and the United States. His versatile skill is apparent in such accomplished paintings as the early *Rehearsal of the Pasdeloup Orchestra*, the renowned *Madame X*, and his sensitive portrait of *Mrs. Fiske Warren and Her Daughter* (cat. nos. 68, 69, 70). Mary Cassatt, an independent young lady from Philadelphia, became an important member of the French Impressionist group, and was also highly influential in early acceptance of Impressionism by American collectors. James Abbott McNeill Whistler, who was born in Lowell, Mass., absorbed in Paris Impressionist freedom of color, but, also influenced by the vogue for *japonisme*, later developed a highly refined style which in principle approached abstraction. Operating under his aesthetic premise of "art for art's sake," his compositions became sensitively ordered tonal harmonies.

In the last quarter of the century, Impressionism was the dominant influence on American painters. Of the uncounted artists who adopted Impressionist styles, Childe Hassam, John Twachtman and later the influential teacher William Merritt Chase were leading exponents. Hassam's rapid and successful transition to Impressionism can be seen in two major pictures, the naturalist view of *Boston Common at Twilight* (cat. no. 74) of 1886 and the vibrantly colorful *Grand Prix Day* (cat. no. 75) painted in Paris a year later. In his superb *Arques-La-Bataille* (cat. no. 76), Twachtman on the other hand adapted Impressionist awareness of light and atmosphere to his own poetic style.

In the first decade of the twentieth century, a rebellious spirit arose in the industrial, urban centers of the East. Disgusted with the artificiality of academic formulas and the increasing repetition and irrelevance of the Impressionists, several young artists in Philadelphia and then New York resolved to revitalize Realism in American painting. The initial group, led by the articulate teacher, Robert Henri, included John Sloan, George Luks and William Glackens. They shared a common apprenticeship under Thomas Anshutz, Eakins' pupil, at the Pennsylvania Academy and experience as newspaper illustrators. Under Henri's lead, they insisted that true reality lay in the streets, saloons and surroundings of the city. Joined by such diverse painters as Maurice Prendergast, Arthur B. Davies, Everett Shinn and Ernest Lawson, at their first exhibition in 1908 the Eight (dubbed the Ashcan School) outraged the public and critics with bluntly direct scenes of back street city life. As appears in Sloan's *Pigeons* (cat. no. 78), their radical aspect lay less in style than in subject.

The famous Armory Show of 1913, organized largely by Arthur B. Davies, then staggered Americans with its revelations of the revolutionary developments of recent European art, especially Post-Impressionism, Constructivism and early Cubism. Many young painters immediately experimented in the new styles, and international contacts rapidly increased. Marsden Hartley, a powerfully intro-spective artist from Maine, had already absorbed in France elements of Symbolist art, and later under the influence of Cubism and German Expressionism created some of his most impressive works. The Italian immigrant, Joseph Stella, main-tained close contacts with Europe and successively experimented with Cubism, Orphism and Italian Futurism, aspects of which appear in his shimmering painting, *Coney Island* (cat. no. 84) of about 1915. Stuart Davis was attracted briefly to the concentrated forms and arbitrary color of Van Gogh and Gauguin, both represented in the Armory Show. He later was one of the earliest American abstractionists, basing his art on Cubism, and was an influential friend of the Abstract Expres-sionists.

In the twenties and thirties, Realism was reaffirmed as a major current particu-larly through the work of George Bellows, Edward Hopper and Walt Kuhn. Bellows, a pupil of Henri, ordered his Realism on the geometric principles of Dynamic Symmetry, achieving as in his *Emma and Her Children* (cat. no. 81) a forceful clarity of structure and monumental form. Hopper remained independent of modernist styles and continued the nineteenth century tradition of objective realism. Yet, as in *Room in Brooklyn* (cat. no. 82), his strong color and sure economy of statement achieved a telling formal and emotional impact of loneliness and isolation. Others, such as the Precisionists, Charles Demuth and Charles Sheeler, approached ab-straction from Realist origins through isolation and intensification of objective observation. Sheeler especially developed a starkly powerful style from the pur-poseful clarity of industrial forms. Still other manifestations of Realist technique appear in the constructions of Edwin Dickinson, the abstracted naturalism of Milton Avery, Andrew Wyeth's concentrated representationalism and even Pop Art's patent assimilation of everyday images.

A critical point in the course of American painting occurred in the forties with the radical reorientation of advanced art toward abstraction. The Depression of the thirties, the emigration to the United States of leading European artists, and the disruptive hiatus of the war all contributed to an aesthetic revolution in postwar America. Interruption of established patterns allowed greater receptivity to earlier developments of modern European art. The new concentration of progressive European ideas helped to establish New York as the vital center of world art. From this ferment Jackson Pollock rose as the pioneering figure of a radically different and dynamic concept of abstraction. Stimulated by his example, a group of painters was formed sharing similar ideas but embracing widely differing styles. They have been variously identified as Abstract Expressionists, action painters or by the more encompassing term, the New York school. Partly guided by his involvement in European expressionism and Surrealist automatism, Pollock had developed a style which denied traditional concepts of space and form, eliminated references to external images and asserted the artist's immediate involvement in the act of creation of his work. Of the painters associated with the group, Willem de Kooning and Franz Kline were closest in spirit to Pollock's Abstract Expressionism. Both *Easter Monday* (cat. no. 95) by de Kooning and *Probst I* (cat. no. 96) by Kline exclaim the explosive immediacy of the artist's hand and achieve the composition totally through abstract formal means. Unlike Pollock, both utilize a personal vocabulary of geometric shapes, de Kooning's in characteristically vivid colors, and Kline's almost exclusively in resonant contrasts of black and white.

Robert Motherwell and Adolph Gottlieb represent two more facets of the Abstract Expressionist spectrum. The mature work of both is characterized by large scale, simplified shapes or areas of color, in which composition is structured and controlled. Motherwell's *Elegy to the Spanish Republic, 70* (cat. no. 98), from his monumental series of that title, resembles Kline in its emphasis on black and white yet remains more strictly ordered. Control and balance are central to Gottlieb's *Thrust* (cat. no. 97), from his "Burst" series, which concentrates on the relationship of two basic symbols, strongly contrasting in mood, that hover in a field of color.

While the Abstract Expressionists dominated public attention in the forties and fifties, a concurrent development of abstraction along formal and often geometric lines also existed. It appeared in the sixties in such various styles as abstract imagist painting, minimal, hard-edge, color-field, optical and kinetic, and Pop art. Hard-edge painting strove for a purity and unity of statement through clearly defined unmodulated areas of color. *Blue Red Green* (cat. no. 99) by Ellsworth Kelly, a pioneer of the movement, achieves fluid articulation of the composition through the interralationship of only a few carefully selected colors and shapes.

Color-field painting has been one of the most significant developments of the generative Abstract Expressionist period. Originating in experiments by Helen Frankenthaler in the early fifties, and advanced by Morris Louis, Kenneth Noland, Jules Olitski and Frank Stella up to the present, color-field painting is perhaps the most important pictorial form of the past two decades. Frankenthaler had perceived new implications in Pollock's work. By staining color directly into raw canvas, eliminating texture and making the design and its format one, she further emphasized the surface plane as opposed to a pictorial space. In recent years, she has developed toward larger scale with fewer color shapes. In *Stride* (cat. no.100) of 1969, the composition is confined to a few basic monumental shapes in a single color. The viewer enters a vast picture world which seems to extend limitlessly beyond the canvas edge.

The progress of American painting from early portrait formulas to the intellectually challenging art of today has been marked by increasingly swift change. As today's artists often blur or deny traditional forms of art in a search for more personal meaning, time is essential to assess the art of our age. It is emphatically clear however that through three centuries, American painters have established a unique national tradition marked throughout by works of the highest quality.

Explanations

Virtually all works lent by the Museum of Fine Arts, Boston, are catalogued extensively either in the recently published *American Paintings in the Museum of Fine Arts, Boston,* Boston (New York Graphic Society), 2 vols., 1969, or in the catalogue of the *M. and M. Karolik Collection of American Paintings,* Boston and Cambridge (Harvard University Press), 1949. Works lent by the Metropolitan Museum of Art, New York, painted prior to approximately 1860, are discussed at length in Albert T. E. Gardner and Stuart P. Feld, *American Paintings, I: Painters born by 1815,* New York (New York Graphic Society), 1965. No entry in the present catalogue contains references to either the Boston general catalogue or Volume I in the Metropolitan series of catalogues. Specific references are made, however, to entries in the *Karolik Collection* catalogue and to those twentieth-century paintings from the Metropolitan Museum collection that are discussed by Henry Geldzahler in his *American Painting in the 20th Century,* New York (New York Graphic Society), 1965.

While the complete history of ownership of paintings is recorded when available, except when possession is directly through family descent, references to exhibitions and publications are limited to the few most important, recent or generally available ones. Names of museums and titles are usually abbreviated. Full references may be found in the Bibliography at the back, together with additional general references on the artists or broader aspects of American painting.

Height precedes width in all instances. The order of entries and illustrations is arranged generally along chronological lines, with minor exception made to group together works of a similar type which may vary somewhat in date.

Catalogue

ANONYMOUS, Seventeenth Century

1

Robert Gibbs

Oil on canvas. 40 x 33 inches.
Dated upper right: *AE. 4½. A° 1670.*
Robert Gibbs (1665–1702), a wealthy Boston merchant like his father, settled in Salem in 1690 and two years later married Mary Shrimpton of Boston. This portrait and the pendants of his brother Henry and sister Margaret (privately owned) are among the finest of the perhaps two dozen surviving seventeenth-century American paintings. The artist was almost certainly the so-called Freake Limner, named for his famous portraits of *John Freake* and *Mrs. Freake and Baby Mary* (Worcester Art Museum). In sharp outline and meticulous detail these paintings recall the Netherlandish and Tudor English style of the previous century. Yet the absence of seventeenth-century counterparts suggests that the artist was an emigrant provincial English house painter who, with skill beyond his experience, sought to satisfy the growing market for portraits, using his recollections of earlier English paintings as models.

Collection:
Theron J. Damon, direct descendant of the subject.
Museum of Fine Arts, Boston. M. and M. Karolik Fund, 1969.

Exhibitions:
Worcester, Mass., Art Museum, *XVIIth Century Painting in New England*, 1934, p. 89, repr. p. 88; New York, Metropolitan Museum, *Life in America*, 1939, no. 3, repr. p. 3; Boston, MFA, *Centennial Acquisitions: Art Treasures for Tomorrow*, 1970, p. 106, no. 72, repr.

Bibliography:
A. Burroughs, *Limners and Likenesses*, Cambridge, Mass., 1936, pp. 9–11, repr. p. 5.

JOHN SMIBERT (1688–1751)

Born in Edinburgh, Scotland, Smibert was apprenticed to a house painter there until his departure for London in 1709. After formal training at the Great Queen Street Academy, he returned to Edinburgh to work as a portrait painter. From 1719 to 1722 he studied in Italy, principally copying old masters, then worked in London as a busy if not important portraitist until the fall of 1728. The opportunity for greater success encouraged him to accompany Dean George Berkeley to Newport, R. I., on the latter's ultimately fruitless mission to found a college for the Indians in Bermuda. Smibert, however, left Newport for Boston late in 1729, opened an artist's supply shop, and was immediately successful. As the only trained artist in the colony, except for the engraver Peter Pelham, his portraits in the manner of Sir Godfrey Kneller set the style of the time.

2

Francis Brinley

Oil on canvas. 50 x 39¼ inches.
Painted in 1729.
Francis Brinley (1690–1765) moved to America from England in 1710 on the promise of a large inheritance by his grandfather. First in Newport, R. I., he later settled in Boston where he married Deborah Lyde (no. 3) in 1718. His grandfather's death the next year brought him a substantial fortune, including a tract of high land in Roxbury overlooking Boston. Brinley was an important figure in the life of Boston and frequently host to visiting dignitaries. The landscape background, not the usual imaginary view, is perhaps the earliest view of Boston, probably as seen from Datchett House, Brinley's stately home.

1 ANONYMOUS. Robert Gibbs

2 SMIBERT. Francis Brinley

23

3 SMIBERT. Mrs. Francis Brinley and Her Infant Son

Collections:
Descendants of the subject.
The Metropolitan Museum of Art, New York.
Rogers Fund, 1962.
Exhibitions:
New York, Metropolitan Museum, *The Hudson-Fulton Celebration*, 1909, no. 35; New Haven, Yale University Art Gallery, *The Smibert Tradition*, 1949, no. 5.
Bibliography:
H. W. Foote, *John Smibert*, Cambridge, Mass., 1950, pp. 64, 136; S. P. Feld, "In the Latest London Manner," *Metropolitan Museum Bulletin,* May, 1963, pp. 296–308, repr. p. 298.

JOHN SMIBERT
3
Mrs. Francis Brinley and Her Infant Son

Oil on canvas. 50 x 39¼ inches.
Painted in 1729, pendant to the preceding.

Deborah Lyde Brinley (1698–1761), was a granddaughter of the famous political figure, Judge Nathaniel Byfield, son-in-law of Governor Leverett. Of her seven children, the one in the portrait usually had been identified as Henry or Edward, from a stylistic dating of 1731. In his recently discovered *Journal,* Smibert called the child Francis, and gave the painting's date as 1729, only a few months after his arrival in America. As in the portrait of Mr. Brinley, the composition derives from several English mezzotints. A frequent source for Colonial artists, Smibert owned – and sold – a great many. Both portraits are vigorously painted and are among his finest achievements.

Collections:
Descendants of the subject.
The Metropolitan Museum of Art, New York.
Rogers Fund, 1962.
Exhibitions:
New York, Metropolitan Museum, *The Hudson-Fulton Celebration*, 1909, no. 36; New Haven, Yale University Art Gallery, *The Smibert Tradition*, 1949, no. 6.
Bibliography:
H. W. Foote, *John Smibert*, Cambridge, Mass., 1950, pp. 64, 137; S. P. Feld, "In the Latest London Manner," *Metropolitan Museum Bulletin*, May, 1963, pp. 296–308, repr. p. 299; D. Evans, J. Kerslake, and A. Oliver, *The Notebook of John Smibert*, Boston, 1969, pp. 21, 87, 104 (also refers to Mr. Brinley).

JOSEPH BLACKBURN
(active before 1752–1778)

Probably born in England, Blackburn's earliest known works of 1752, were painted in Bermuda. He was in Newport in 1754, had established himself in Boston by 1755 and worked primarily there and in the vicinity of Portsmouth, N. H. until 1763. A bill dated 1764 places him in London at that time and dated portraits of 1774 and 1778 suggest that he remained active as a portraitist there. Blackburn's absorption of the rococo portrait style fashionable in mid-century London prior to his coming to America, introduced a highly important new force to American painting.

4
Isaac Winslow and His Family

Oil on canvas. 53½ x 79½ inches.
Signed and dated lower left: *J. Blackburn Pinx. 1755.*

Winslow's first wife Lucy bore him eleven children, five of whom died in infancy. Here she holds baby Hannah (1755–1819), who married John Wall, a Captain in the British Army, in 1778. On the right is Lucy Winslow, born in Boston in 1749, who married George Irving, a Boston merchant, in 1768. When she died two years later he married Mary MacIntosh Royall, who is represented in Copley's early masterpiece, *Mary and Elizabeth Royall* (no. 7). The greater elegance and richer color of Blackburn's painting soon replaced the solid baroque tradition in Copley's paintings of the late 1750's. Copley soon outstripped Blackburn and probably contributed to the latter's departure from Boston.

Collections:
Descendants of the subject.
Museum of Fine Arts, Boston. Abraham Shuman Fund, 1942.
Exhibitions:
New York, Metropolitan Museum, *Life in America*, 1939, no. 12, repr. p. 9; Chicago, Art Institute, *From Colony to Nation*, 1949, no. 23, repr.
Bibliography:
O. W. Larkin, *Art and Life in America*, New York, 1949, p. 52, repr.; V. Barker, *American Painting*, New York, 1950, p. 110, fig. 16.

ROBERT FEKE
(about 1705–after 1750)

One of the most enigmatic of eighteenth-century American painters, Feke was probably born in Oyster Bay, New York. Except for the apparent influence of John Smibert, nothing is known of his artistic training. His earliest known and most ambitious work, the signed and dated *Family of Isaac Royall* (Harvard University Law School), places him in Boston in 1741. Other dated works locate him primarily in Newport, R. I., but also in Philadelphia and again in Boston before he disappeared from record after 1750. Despite lack of formal training, the skillful sophistication of his portraits confirms him as one of the finest American painters of the period.

5
Isaac Winslow

Oil on canvas. 50 x 40 inches.
Painted about 1748.

4   BLACKBURN. Isaac Winslow and His Family

Facing page
5   FEKE. Isaac Winslow

Isaac Winslow (1707–1777) was a partner with his brother Joshua in a profitable Boston shipping and mercantile business. In 1747, he married Lucy, daughter of General Samuel Waldo; following her death, he married Jemima Debuke in 1770. A Loyalist, he fled to Halifax, N. S., on the British evacuation of Boston in 1776 and died there. The accomplished grace and fresh color of the painting caused it to be attributed to Copley until the 1930's.

Collections:
Descendants of the subject.
Museum of Fine Arts, Boston. Gift in memory of the sitter's granddaughter, Mary Russell Winslow Bradford, by her great-grandson, Russell Wiles, 1942.

Exhibitions:
New York, Whitney Museum, Huntington, N.Y., Heckscher Museum, and Boston, MFA, *Robert Feke*, 1946, no. 30, repr.; London, Tate Gallery, *American Painting*, 1946, no. 84.

Bibliography:
B. N. Parker, "A Member of the Winslow Family in Boston," *Boston MFA Bulletin*, 1942, XL, no. 241, repr. p. 87.

JOSEPH BADGER (1708–1765)

Born in Charlestown, Mass., Badger was a house and sign painter and glazier by trade. Yet, despite his production of perhaps one hundred portraits, little is known of his life. After about 1740 he was painting portraits in Boston and the surrounding communities. His works were not identified until 1917, and had often been attributed to Smibert, Blackburn and Copley. Smibert's death in 1751 and Blackburn's departure for England made him one of the principal portraitists of Boston.

6
James Badger
Oil on canvas. $42^{1}/_{2}$ x $33^{1}/_{8}$ inches.

Dated on the back: *July 8th 1760*. The naive charm of Badger's portrait of his grandson James (1757–1817) makes it one of his most appealing works. A segment of the inscription on James Badger's tombstone in Charleston, S.C., where he had moved in 1777 sums up his life: "In the year 1788 he was chosen clerk of the Archdale Independent Church and for 30 years ably & faithfully discharged the duties of that office. As a member of this community he was useful, as a husband tender, as a Father affectionate, as a master indulgent, and as a friend sincere. As a Teacher of Sacred Music he indefatigably laboured to promote that useful science."

Collections:
Descendants of the subject.
The Metropolitan Museum of Art, New York. Rogers Fund, 1929.

Exhibitions:
New-York Historical Society, *Up from the Cradle (Early American Portraits of Children)*, 1948–1949, no. 10.

Bibliography:
J. T. Flexner, *First Flowers of Our Wilderness*, Boston, 1947, pp. 198 f., 344.

JOHN SINGLETON COPLEY (1738–1815)

Copley was born probably in Boston, the son of recent immigrants from Ireland. His father, a tobacconist, died a few years after his birth. In 1748, his mother married the English trained painter and engraver, Peter Pelham, who introduced the boy to the arts. With Pelham's and John Smibert's death three years later, Copley was left to train himself by studying their work and later that of Greenwood, Feke, and Blackburn. Guided by intuitive genius and his determinedly objective eye, Copley soon surpassed all his sources

and achieved an artistic pre-eminence unmatched for a century. For years the finest artist in America, he was anxious to compare himself with the famed London portraitists, and in 1774 embarked on a study tour of Italy, then settled in London. As part of the American colony centered around the expatriate Benjamin West, he soon attempted historical painting but also remained active as a portraitist in London until his death.

7
Mary and Elizabeth Royall
Oil on canvas. $57^{1}/_{2}$ x 48 inches.
Painted about 1758.

The rococo delicacy and bright color of this early masterpiece, painted when Copley was only twenty, owe much to Blackburn, to whom it was attributed until the 1930's. Yet the graceful solution of the difficult double portrait composition and the technical virtuosity excel anything Copley had seen before. Mary MacIntosh and Elizabeth Royall were daughters of the wealthy Medford merchant and landowner, Isaac Royall. Mary (1745–1786) married George Irving, a Tory merchant, in 1775. They fled Washington's siege of Boston going to London via Halifax, N. S. in 1776. Elizabeth (1747–1775) married William Pepperell Sparhawk (later Sir William Pepperell, Bart.), but died during the siege.

Collections:
The Royall family, Medford, Mass., until 1779; Gideon Snow, Boston; Rev. Theodore Snow, Boston; H. Elizabeth Snow, Pomfret, Conn.
Museum of Fine Arts, Boston. Julia Knight Fox Fund, 1925.

Exhibitions:
Washington, National Gallery, New York, Metropolitan Museum, and Boston, MFA, *Copley*, 1965–1966, no. 9, pl. I; New York,

6   BADGER. James Badger

7 COPLEY. Mary and Elizabeth Royall

Metropolitan Museum, *100 Paintings from the Boston Museum*, 1970.

Bibliography:
E. P. Richardson, *Painting in America*, New York, 1956, p. 72, fig. 24; J. D. Prown, *Copley*, Cambridge, Mass., 1966, I, p. 31, fig. 83, II, p. 22.

JOHN SINGLETON COPLEY
8
Nicholas Boylston

Oil on canvas. 50¹/₄ x 40¹/₄ inches.
Painted about 1767.

The portrait of Nicholas Boylston (1716–1771) is remarkable both as a brilliant example of Copley's mature portrait style, and for its illustration of his device of the informal formal portrait. Boylston, a wealthy merchant and important benefactor of Harvard College, is casually posed without a wig, wearing a red turban over his shaved head, and draped in a brown silk banyan or dressing gown. Copley's tour de force of shimmering textures and rich colors reveals his complete command of his craft.

Collections:
Moses Kimball, Boston, by 1873; David P. Kimball, Boston.
Museum of Fine Arts, Boston. Bequest of David P. Kimball, 1923.

Exhibitions:
Paris, Musée du Jeu de Paume, *Trois Siècles d'Art aux Etats-Unis*, 1938, no. 30, pl. 2; London, Tate Gallery, *American Painting*, 1946, no. 45.

Bibliography:
B. N. Parker and A. B. Wheeler, *Copley*, Boston, 1938, p. 44, pl. 78; J. D. Prown, *Copley*, Cambridge, Mass., 1966, I, p. 66, fig. 184.

JOHN SINGLETON COPLEY
9
Paul Revere

Oil on canvas. 35 x 28¹/₂ inches.
Painted about 1768–1770.

Copley's portrait of the American patriot Revere (1735–1818), unquestionably one of America's most famous paintings, is of special interest beyond the fame of the subject. Copley presents his contemporary, one of America's finest silversmiths, at work and in shirtsleeves. The informal composition and brilliant translation of gleaming silver and polished mahogany establish Copley's affinities with the great seventeenth-century Dutch realists, who also painted for a wealthy merchant society. Although the charming and versatile Revere is most famous for his legendary ride of April 19, 1775, in addition to silversmithing, he made engravings, designed and printed paper currency, built a gunpowder plant, a foundry for church bells, a copper rolling mill and even made false teeth.

Collections:
Descendants of the subject.
Museum of Fine Arts, Boston. Gift of Joseph W., William B., and Edward H. R. Revere, 1930.

Exhibitions:
Washington, National Gallery, New York, Metropolitan Museum, and Boston, MFA, *Copley*, 1965–1966, no. 45, repr. p. 65; New York, Metropolitan Museum, *100 Paintings from the Boston Museum*, 1970.

Bibliography:
B. N. Parker and A. B. Wheeler, *Copley*, Boston, 1938, pp. 160–161, pl. 63; E. Forbes, *Paul Revere and the World He Lived In*, Cambridge, Mass., 1942, pp. 55, 112–114, repr. frontispiece; J. D. Prown, *Copley*, Cambridge, Mass., 1966, I, pp. 74–75, fig. 272.

JOHN SINGLETON COPLEY
10
Mrs. Richard Skinner

Oil on canvas. 39³/₄ x 30³/₄ inches.
Signed and dated center right: *John Singleton Copley pinx/1772/Boston*.

In his portraits of women, whether of

8 COPLEY. Nicholas Boylston

9 COPLEY. Paul Revere

10 COPLEY. Mrs. Richard Skinner

the charming Royall children, or of fashionable ladies, Copley is at his best. Here, the decorative clothing and delicate features and fingers, reflected in the polished surface of the mahogany table, form a visual feast that is still essentially American in its unflattering truth to life. Dorothy Wendell Skinner (1733–1822), married her stepbrother, Richard Skinner of Marblehead, in 1756. She was also first cousin of Dorothy Quincy, wife of John Hancock, whose portrait by Copley (Boston MFA) is nearly identical.

Collections:
Lord Lyndhurst, the artist's son, London; *Lyndhurst Sale*, Christie's, London, March 5, 1864, no. 60 (as *Portrait of a Lady*); Mrs. Martin Brimmer, great-granddaughter of the artist, Boston.
Museum of Fine Arts, Boston. Bequest of Mrs. Martin Brimmer, 1906.

Exhibitions:
Baltimore Museum of Art, *The Age of Elegance: Rococo and Its Effect*, 1959, no. 416; Washington, National Gallery, New York, Metropolitan Museum, and Boston, MFA, *Copley,* 1965–1966, no. 50, pl. IX.

Bibliography:
B. N. Parker and A. B. Wheeler, *Copley,* Boston, 1938, pp. 182–183, pl. 119; J. D. Prown, *Copley,* Cambridge, Mass., 1966, I, p. 85, fig. 315.

JOHN SINGLETON COPLEY
11

Watson and the Shark

Oil on canvas. 72 x 90¼ inches.
Signed and dated inside the stern of the boat: *J. S. Copley P. 1778.*
This dramatic and revolutionary painting is Copley's earliest major attempt at history painting. He has extended West's concept of depicting contemporary events in contemporary dress, such as *The Death of General Wolfe* of 1770 (National Gallery of Canada, Ottawa),

by painting not a commander's heroic demise but a shark's attack on a young boy. In concept, his painting anticipated by forty years Theodore Géricault's celebrated *Raft of the Medusa* (Louvre). Brooke Watson, later a prosperous merchant and Lord Mayor of London, when a youthful midshipman was attacked by a shark while swimming in Havana Harbor. Copley chose the critical moment – the gaping jaws of the shark, the outstretched hands, the poised boathook – and created a monumental scene of dramatic action unprecedented in American painting. The painting is an exact replica, painted in the same year, of the original version commissioned by Watson in the National Gallery of Art, Washington.

Collections:
Lord Lyndhurst, the artist's son, London; *Lyndhurst Sale*, Christie's, London, March 5, 1864, no. 61; Charles Hook Appleton, Boston, 1864; Mrs. George von Lengerke Meyer, his daughter, 1882.
Museum of Fine Arts, Boston. Gift of Mrs. George von Lengerke Meyer, 1889.

Exhibitions:
New York, Museum of Modern Art, *Romantic Painting in America*, 1943, pp. 8–9, no. 57, repr. p. 49; Washington, National Gallery, New York, Metropolitan Museum, and Boston, MFA, *Copley,* 1965–1966, no. 68 b, repr. p. 94.

Bibliography:
E. P. Richardson, "Watson and the Shark by Copley," *Art Quarterly,* 1947, X, no. 3, pp. 213, 218, (note 2), fig. 3; J. D. Prown, *Copley,* Cambridge, Mass., 1966, II, pp. 267, 268, 270–275, fig. 372.

JOHN SINGLETON COPLEY
12

Midshipman Augustus Brine

Oil on canvas. 50 x 40 inches.
Signed and dated left center: *J. S. Copley Pin/1782.*

11 COPLEY. Watson and the Shark

12 COPLEY. Midshipman Augustus Brine

Augustus Brine (1770–1840), son of Admiral James Brine and his first wife, Jane Knight, enlisted at the age of twelve in the British Navy and served as a midshipman aboard his father's ship, the *Belliqueux*. He was in command of the *Medway* in 1805 against Napoleon's attempted invasion of England, and on the same vessel, in 1814, captured the American brig-of-war *Syran* off the African coast. In this painting, six brief years after Copley arrived in England, he reveals his brilliant adaptability to the freer bravura style of his English colleagues.

Collections:
Descendants of the subject, Lymington, Hampshire; Mrs. Knapton, sold Christie's, London, Dec. 12, 1924, no. 111; Richard de Wolfe Brixey.
The Metropolitan Museum of Art, New York. Bequest of Richard de Wolfe Brixey, 1943.

Exhibitions:
Washington, National Gallery, New York, Metropolitan Museum, and Boston, MFA, *Copley*, 1965–1966, pp. 100, 140, no. 75, color pl. XIII; Boston, MFA, *Masterpieces of Painting in the Metropolitan Museum*, 1970.

Bibliography:
J. D. Prown, *Copley*, Cambridge, Mass., 1966, II, pp. 294, 295, 345, 413, fig. 423.

CHARLES WILLSON PEALE (1741–1827)

Born in Queen Anne County, Md., Peale was first a saddler and silversmith in Annapolis, but soon attempted painting, receiving lessons from John Hesselius. In 1765, he visited Boston where he saw the paintings in Smibert's old studio, and also met Copley who strongly influenced his style. From 1767 to 1769, Peale spent two years under West in London. On his return he became increasingly active in Annapolis and especially in Philadelphia where he settled in 1778. Although a prolific artist – over 1,000 paintings are recorded – his later years were devoted to a multitude of projects: inventions, writings on health, happiness, and bridge building, and especially his own museum, established in 1782. There he assembled side by side his own paintings, prints, mounted birds and animals, and various curiosities including a mastodon skeleton which he had helped to excavate. Peale was the most important portraitist of colonial Philadelphia, and his large family also included a number of outstanding artists.

13
Mrs. Samuel Mifflin and her Granddaughter Rebecca Mifflin Francis
Oil on canvas. 49³/₄ x 39³/₄ inches.
Painted about 1780.
The portrait of Rebecca Edghill Mifflin, wife of a successful Philadelphia businessman and public figure, whose portrait is also in the Metropolitan Museum, personifies the domestic virtues of her day. She and her granddaughter, dressed in their finest, are captured in a delightful moment of family tranquillity reflecting the text she holds on "FELIAL LOVE" and "Duty."

Collections:
Descendants of Samuel Mifflin.
The Metropolitan Museum of Art, New York. Egleston Fund, 1922.

Exhibition:
Philadelphia Academy, *Portraits by Charles Willson Peale, James Peale, and Rembrandt Peale*, 1923, no. 169.

Bibliography:
C. C. Sellers, *Portraits and Miniatures by Charles Willson Peale*, Philadelphia, 1952, p. 142, no. 548.

RALPH EARL (1751–1801)

Earl was born in Worcester County, Mass., but little is known of his life before he opened a studio in New Haven, Conn. in 1775. A Loyalist, he left for England in 1778 and until 1785 he worked there under Benjamin West, also succeeding in exhibiting paintings at the Royal Academy. After returning to America, he painted a number of bold and vigorous portraits from Vermont to New York, but especially in Connecticut, until his death "of intemperance" in Bolton, Conn. His style, initially based on Copley's, is usually monumental in scale and is a powerfully direct and simplied statement.

14
Mrs. Noah Smith and Her Children
Oil on canvas. 64 x 85³/₄ inches.
Signed and dated lower left: *Ralph Earl pinxit 1798.*
Among the finest and most ambitious of Earl's group portraits, this work was painted in Bennington, Vermont late in his career. Chloe Burrall Smith was the wife of a man active in the political life of Vermont, whose portrait (Art Institute of Chicago) Earl also painted. She is grandly posed with her children, Henry, Daniel, Noah, Jr., Eliza, and Celia. Daniel became a missionary in Natchez, Tennessee, Mississippi, and Kentucky; Noah, Jr. became a teacher in Natchez.

Collections:
Descendants of Eliza Smith until 1958; Edgar William and Bernice Chrysler Garbisch.
The Metropolitan Museum of Art, New York. Gift of Edgar William and Bernice Chrysler Garbisch, 1964.

Exhibitions:
New York, Metropolitan Museum (1961–1962) and American Federation of Arts (circulating exhibition), *101 Masterpieces of American Primitive Painting from the Collection of Edgar William and Bernice*

13 PEALE. Mrs. Samuel Mifflin and Her Granddaughter Rebecca Mifflin Francis

14 EARL. Mrs. Noah Smith and Her Children

15 HATHAWAY. Lady with Her Pets

Chrysler Garbisch, 1962–1964, p.144, no.31, color pl.31.

Bibliography:
S. P. F(eld), "Note," *Metropolitan Museum Bulletin*, April, 1965, p.300.

RUFUS HATHAWAY
(about 1770–1822)

Like many of the naive American artists, little is known of Hathaway's life. Supposedly born in Freetown, Mass., he was an itinerant artist. His earliest known work, shown here, is of 1790. On a painting trip to Duxbury, Mass., in 1795, he met and married Judith Winsor, daughter of a prominent merchant. Persuaded by his father-in-law to undertake a more stable profession, Hathaway studied medicine, became Duxbury's only doctor and abandoned painting except for occasional portraits of friends.

15
Lady with Her Pets

Oil on canvas. 34$\frac{1}{4}$ x 32 inches.
Signed and dated lower right: *RH/Oct^r/1790*. Inscribed lower left: *Canter*.
The sitter is possibly Molly Whales Leonard of Marshfield, Mass., but much of the painting's delight is in the extraordinary assemblage of brightly colored and decoratively patterned birds and insects, and the cat, probably named Canter. The painting is one of the finest in the important tradition of works by talented but untrained artists which flourished especially in New England, until largely replaced by the camera in the late nineteenth century.

Collections:
Mary Allis, Fairfield, Conn.; Edgar William and Bernice Chrysler Garbisch.
The Metropolitan Museum of Art, New York. Gift of Edgar William and Bernice Chrysler Garbisch, 1963.

Exhibitions:
American Federation of Arts (circulating exhibition), *American Naive Painting of the 18th and 19th Centuries, 111 Masterpieces from the Collection of Edgar William and Bernice Chrysler Garbisch*, 1969, pp.140, 147, no.23, color pl.23; Osaka, Japan, Expo 70, United States Pavilion, 1970.

Bibliography:
N. F. Little, "Dr. Rufus Hathaway...," *Art in America*, 1953, XLI, no.3, pp.95 f.

EDWARD HICKS (1780–1849)

Perhaps the most eagerly admired of American primitive painters today, Edward Hicks, born in rural Newtown, Pa., as a child was placed with a Quaker family following his mother's early death and father's later poverty. Little interested in education, he was apprenticed to a coachmaker at thirteen. By 1810, he was an extremely popular decorator of shop signs and household utensils, often embellishing them with historical or scriptural subjects. Always active as a Quaker, while continuing ornamental painting, he also produced a great many replicas of several favorite, usually symbolic, themes, of which *The Peaceable Kingdom* is one of the best known.

16
The Falls of Niagara

Oil on canvas. 31$\frac{1}{2}$ x 38 inches.
Painted probably after 1820.
Paintings and prints of Niagara abounded in nineteenth century America. Each artist recorded his personal experience of the drama of this natural wonder. Hicks, who visited the Falls in 1819, has included their grandeur as part of a more general evocation of the harmony and beauty of God's world. The poem around the margin is excerpted from *The Foresters*, a long narrative poem by

The Falls

'f Niagara

Above, below, where'er the astonished eye
Turns to behold, new opening wonders lie,

With uproar hideous first the *falls* appear,
The stunning tumult thundering on the ear.

This great o'erwhelming work of awful Time
In all its dread magnificence sublime

Rises on our view, amid a crashing roar
That bids us kneel, and Time's great God adore.

18   25

16 HICKS. The Falls of Niagara
17 WEST. Moses Viewing the Promised Land

Alexander Wilson, the famous American ornithologist and artist.

Collection:
Edgar William and Bernice Chrysler Garbisch. The Metropolitan Museum of Art, New York. Gift of Edgar William and Bernice Chrysler Garbisch, 1962.

Exhibitions:
American Federation of Arts (circulating exhibition), *American Naive Painting of the 18th and 19th Centuries, 111 Masterpieces from the Collection of Edgar William and Bernice Chrysler Garbisch*, 1969, pp. 140–141, 149, no. 42, pl. 42; Osaka, Japan, Expo 70, United States Pavilion, 1970.

Bibliography:
A. Ford, *Edward Hicks, Painter of the Peaceable Kingdom*, Philadelphia, 1952, pp. 32 f.

BENJAMIN WEST (1738–1820)

Although born in the present Swarthmore, Pa., son of an innkeeper, West was destined to be a pivotal figure of the Anglo-American art world. A prodigy, he drew and painted by eight and was a sign and portrait painter in Philadelphia by 1756. Patrons sponsored a trip to Italy in 1759; three years of study in Florence, Rome, and Venice immersed him in the new Neoclassic movement inspired by the discoveries at Paestum, Pompeii, and Herculaneum. In London in 1762, his great charm and novelty won such immediate success that he settled there. He then introduced a novel approach to historical and allegorical painting—moralizing subjects in the grand manner, strikingly new for their realism and strict adherence to the vocabulary of antiquity. His paintings of modern history in contemporary dress, not the traditional togas, were equally radical. As historical painter to King George III and President of the Royal Academy, his influence as an artist was extensive. Yet of greater importance was his unfailing assistance and instruction to the many American artists attracted to his studio.

17
Moses Viewing the Promised Land
Oil on panel. 19³/₄ x 28³/₄ inches. Signed and dated bottom center: *B. West 1801*
This splendid painting is one of a great many studies for a never finished series of decorations for the Royal chapel at Windsor. The project, begun in 1780 and abandoned in 1801, involved thirty-six religious subjects, half from the Old Testament and half from the New, for a series on "Revealed Religion." In baroque drama and rich color, the painting recalls both Rubens and seventeenth-century Italian art, sources which West often consulted.

Collections:
With the artist and his family; *Pictures by West sold by George Robins*, London, May 22, 1829, no. 29.
The Metropolitan Museum of Art, New York. Gift of Mr. and Mrs. James W. Fosburgh, by exchange, 1969.

Exhibitions:
London, Royal Academy, *Thirty-third Exhibition*, 1801, no. 243; New York, M. Knoedler and Co., *American Paintings 1750–1950*, 1969, no. 6.

Bibliography:
J. Galt, *West*, London, 1820, II, pp. 51–56, 211, 218, 230.

MATTHEW PRATT (1734–1805)

Pratt was born in Philadelphia. Following an apprenticeship with his uncle, James Claypoole learning sign painting, he worked as a portraitist from 1758 to 1764. The presence of his fellow Philadelphian, Benjamin West, in London drew him there. One of West's first pupils, he studied with him for more than two years, then returned permanently to Philadelphia in 1768, where he continued to paint portraits until his death.

18
The American School
Oil on canvas. 36 x 50¹/₄ inches. Signed and dated, lower left of the painting on the easel: *M. Pratt/ad. 1765*.
Although accomplished as a portraitist, Matthew Pratt is secure in the history of American painting for his ambitious conversation piece documenting West's London studio. West's leadership of the London art world and willing instruction to students offered exposure to the most advanced art circles for numbers of Americans including Copley, Stuart, Trumbull, Charles Willson Peale, Earl, Sully, and Allston. The two figures on the left in the painting are probably West and Pratt.

Collections:
Descendants of the artist; Samuel P. Avery, New York.
The Metropolitan Museum of Art, New York. Gift of Samuel P. Avery, 1897.

Exhibitions:
London, Society of Artists of Great Britain, *Spring Garden Exhibition*, 1766, no. 130; Chicago, Art Institute, *From Colony to Nation*, 1949, no. 96; Boston, MFA, *Masterpieces of Painting in the Metropolitan Museum*, 1970.

Bibliography:
W. Sawitzky, *Matthew Pratt*, New York, 1942, pp. 35 f.

GILBERT STUART (1755–1828)

Stuart grew up in Newport, R. I., and about 1769 became a pupil of the visiting Scottish portraitist, Cosmo Alexander. In 1772 he accompanied Alexander to Edinburgh, but returned almost immediately, after Alexander's death. In

18   PRATT. The American School

London in 1775, Stuart at first had little success but, taken in by West from 1777 to 1782, he swiftly developed his considerable talents, and became a significant competitor with Gainsborough, Reynolds and Romney. Debts from extravagant living drove him first to Dublin and in 1792 to New York. He was warmly received there, then worked in Germantown and Philadelphia until 1803 and in Washington until 1805, after which he settled permanently in Boston. His fluent and sophisticated style, and willing advice to a multitude of young American painters, did much to establish the basic nature of Federal portraiture.

19
Matilda Stoughton de Jaudenes

Oil on canvas. $50^5/_8$ x $39^1/_2$ inches. Painted in 1794.

Matilda Stoughton (1778–after 1822), daughter of John Stoughton, Spanish consul in Boston, at sixteen married Josef de Jaudenes, the ambitious and dashing envoy from Spain to the United States. The portrait, one of a pair painted in the year of her marriage, brilliantly captures the glittering splendor of her finery and jewelry without dominating her youthful beauty. Although the attribution to Stuart was questioned at the time of acquisition by the Metropolitan Museum, perhaps because of the unusually grand treatment of the subject, both paintings are among the finest of Stuart's portraits. The coat of arms and inscription in the upper left are later additions by another hand.

Collections:
The Jaudenes family, Spain.
The Metropolitan Museum of Art, New York. Rogers Fund, 1907.
Exhibitions:
Washington, National Gallery, and Providence, Rhode Island School of Design, *Gilbert Stuart, Portraitist of the Young Republic*, 1967, p. 71, no. 24, repr. p. 70.
Bibliography:
L. Park, *Gilbert Stuart*, New York, 1926, I, p. 433, no. 435.

GILBERT STUART
20
Matthew Clarkson

Oil on canvas. $36^1/_8$ x $28^1/_4$ inches. Painted about 1794.

Matthew Clarkson (1758–1825), of a prominent New York family, served with distinction as aide-de-camp to General Benedict Arnold and later Benjamin Lincoln, Secretary of War. He was later a New York State Senator and President of the Bank of New York. Stuart's painting of his handsome contemporary, done in New York not long after his arrival from Ireland, reveals his assured mastery of the British formal portrait style.

Collections:
Descendants of the subject.
The Metropolitan Museum of Art, New York. Bequest of Helen Shelton Clarkson, 1938.
Exhibitions:
Washington, National Gallery, and Providence, Rhode Island School of Design, *Gilbert Stuart, Portraitist of the Young Republic*, 1967, no. 22, repr. p. 67; Boston, MFA, *Masterpieces of Painting in the Metropolitan Museum*, 1970.
Bibliography:
L. Park, *Gilbert Stuart*, New York, 1926, I, p. 217, no. 159.

GILBERT STUART
21
George Washington

Oil on canvas. $30^1/_4$ x $25^1/_4$ inches. Painted probably in 1795.

Stuart first painted Washington (1732–1799) from life in Philadelphia in 1795, only two years after his arrival from England and Ireland. Known as the "Vaughan" portrait (National Gallery, Washington, D.C.) from its presumed purchase by Washington's friend, Samuel Vaughan, the painting was an immediate success. Of the nearly forty replicas ordered, the so-called Gibbs-Channing-Avery portrait, shown here, is one of the earliest and best. The Vaughan type and the never completed "Athenaeum Head" (Boston Museum, deposited by the Boston Athenaeum), painted from life the next year, of which perhaps seventy-five replicas exist, confirmed Stuart's financial success and permanent popular fame.

Collections:
Col. George Gibbs, New York; Mrs. William Ellery Channing, his sister; William F. Channing, her son, 1858; Samuel P. Avery, 1889; Samuel P. Avery, Jr., 1904.
The Metropolitan Museum of Art, New York. Rogers Fund, 1907.
Exhibitions:
Boston, MFA, *Gilbert Stuart*, 1880, no. 303; New York, Metropolitan Museum, *Life in America*, 1939, no. 38.
Bibliography:
L. Park, *Gilbert Stuart*, New York, 1926, II, pp. 845 f., no. 2.

GILBERT STUART
22
Bishop Jean-Louis Lefebvre de Cheverus

Oil on canvas. $36^1/_4$ x $28^1/_2$ inches. Painted in 1823.

Jean-Louis Anne Magdeleine Lefebvre de Cheverus (1768–1836) was born in Mayenne, France. In 1792 he fled the French Revolution to England and in 1796 was dispatched to assist the Roman Catholic parish in Boston. In 1810 he was consecrated first Bishop of Boston. Intelligent, enthusiastic and tireless, he won admirers of all faiths. On his call to the Bishopric of Montauban

19 STUART. Matilda Stoughton de Jaudenes

20 STUART. Matthew Clarkson

21 STUART George Washington

22 STUART. Bishop Jean-Louis Lefebvre de Cheverus

in 1823, Mrs. John Gore, a member of a patrician Boston family, commissioned the portrait. Shortly before his death, Bishop de Cheverus was elevated to the College of Cardinals. Although a very late work, Stuart has captured the spirit of his subject with exceptional richness and *élan*.

Collections:

Mrs. John Gore, Boston; Mrs. Horatio Greenough, her daughter, Boston, 1836; Mrs. Charlotte Hervoches du Quilliou, her daughter, La Tour de Peilz, Switzerland. Museum of Fine Arts, Boston. Bequest of Mrs. Charlotte Gore Greenough Hervoches du Quilliou, 1921.

Exhibitions:

Boston Athenaeum, *Exhibition*, 1827, no. 118; Boston, MFA, *Gilbert Stuart*, 1880, no. 251; Washington, National Gallery, and Providence, Rhode Island School of Design, *Gilbert Stuart, Portraitist of the Young Republic*, 1967, no. 47, repr. p. 103.

Bibliography:

L. Park, *Gilbert Stuart*, New York, 1926, I, no. 155, repr., III, p. 99.

JAMES PEALE (1749–1831)

The youngest brother of Charles Willson Peale, James was born in Chestertown, Md. He learned saddle-making from his elder brother and was also a cabinet-maker. He also learned to paint from Charles when the latter returned from England in 1769, and after the Revolution they worked closely together, James specializing in miniature portraits. As his eyes began to fail during the 1820's, he turned to painting still life, which remains as a highly important aspect of his work.

23
Balsam Apple and Vegetables

Oil on canvas. $20^{1}/_4$ x $26^{1}/_2$ inches.
Painted after 1820.
Colonial and Federal painting were confined almost exclusively to portraiture, except for historical pictures devoted to the Revolution. James Peale and his nephew Raphaelle were the first to concentrate on still life painting, as well as genre, and were major influences on its development. They transposed the American tradition of realism into these new motifs. This exceptionally fine painting is unusual among Peale's still lifes for its blond palette and casual composition of crisply textured objects.

Collection:

Clifton Peale.
The Metropolitan Museum of Art, New York. Maria DeWitt Jesup Fund, 1939.

Exhibitions:

New York, Century Association, *Paintings by Members of the Peale Family*, 1953, no. 23; New York, Metropolitan Museum, *19th-Century America: Paintings and Sculpture*, 1970, no. 14, repr.

JOHN TRUMBULL (1756–1843)

Trumbull, born in Lebanon, Conn., was the son of the future Revolutionary Governor of the state. Precocious and independent, he graduated from Harvard at seventeen and, overruled in his desire to be an artist, served in the Continental Army drawing maps and sketches of enemy positions. Although once an aide to General Washington, he resigned his commission over a petty dispute, and set out to paint. With West in London in 1780, he was jailed in reprisal for the Major André affair. Although released and deported, he was again with West from 1784 to 1789. In addition to painting portraits, he was inspired by West's and Copley's battle paintings to record pivotal moments of the American Revolution. Those murals, now in the Capitol rotunda in Washington, became the major effort of his career. The dozens of studies for them, many from life, are among his finest works, and uniquely document a momentous period of American history. His later years, during his oppressive Presidency of the American Academy of Arts in New York, were filled with increasing bitterness and controversy.

24
Sortie from Gibraltar

Oil on canvas. 71x107 inches.
Signed and dated lower left: *John Trumbull 1789*.
Painted during his last year in West's studio, the *Sortie* reflects in color, composition, and drama his *Death of General Warren at Bunker Hill* of the Revolutionary series. Trumbull depicted the aftermath of an engagement in the Spanish siege of the British fortress in 1781 in which the British General, Elliot, marched out at night to destroy a line of enemy fortifications. Here Elliot stretches out his hand to the mortally wounded Spanish commander, Don José Barboza, who heroically refuses to surrender.

Collection:

Purchased from the artist by the Boston Athenaeum, 1828.
Museum of Fine Arts, Boston. Deposited by the Boston Athenaeum, 1876.

Exhibitions:

London, Society of Artists of Great Britain, *Spring Garden Exhibition*, 1789; New York, World's Fair, *Masterpieces of Art*, 1939–1940, no. 178, repr. p. 121.

Bibliography:

J. Trumbull, *Reminiscences of His Own Time*, New York, 1841, p. 149; T. Sizer, *Trumbull*, New Haven, 1950, pp. 2, 76.

WASHINGTON ALLSTON (1779–1843)

Allston, born in Georgetown, S.C., was deeply receptive at Harvard to the idealism of early Romanticism. After

23   PEALE. Balsam Apple and Vegetables

24 TRUMBULL. Sortie from Gibraltar

graduation in 1801, he accompanied the miniature painter, Joseph Malbone, to England to study under West. Despite respect for West's ordered Neoclassicism, his spirit responded more to the color and drama of Rubens and the sixteenth-century Venetians seen in the Netherlands and in Paris in 1803. In 1804 he traveled through Italy to Rome where for five years he absorbed the ancient spirit of the city and the new Romantic concepts of Washington Irving and other members of the intellectual community. His work increasingly explored the inner world of fantasy and the imagination. Although in Boston in 1808, he was again in London from 1811 to 1818, then settled permanently in Cambridge, Mass. Widely admired by his American contemporaries, Allston was an influential pioneer of the Romantic tradition in American painting.

25
Moonlit Landscape
Oil on canvas. 24 x 35 inches.
Painted in 1819.
The idyllic calm of the *Moonlit Landscape* is in sharp contrast to the intense drama of the *Elijah* painted only the year before. During the years following his final return from Europe, Allston gave increasingly free rein to his imagination, conceiving nature and man in terms of soft reveries and fantasy. In this particular painting, the art of Claude Lorrain is important, but has been transformed into more idealistic and emotional terms.

Collections:
H. J. Bigelow, Boston, by 1839; Mrs. Jacob Bigelow, Boston, by 1881; William Sturgis Bigelow, Boston.
Museum of Fine Arts, Boston. Gift of William Sturgis Bigelow, 1921.

Exhibitions:
Detroit Institute of Arts and Boston, MFA, *Allston,* 1947, no. 26, repr. p. 30; New York, Metropolitan Museum, *100 Paintings from the Boston Museum,* 1970; New York, Metropolitan Museum, *19th-Century America: Paintings and Sculpture,* 1970, no. 7, repr.
Bibliography:
E. P. Richardson, *Allston,* Chicago, 1948, pp. 144–145, 206, pl. XLVI.

WASHINGTON ALLSTON
26
Elijah in the Desert
Oil on canvas. $48^3/_4$ x $72^1/_2$ inches.
Signed and dated on the back: *W. Allston 1818.*
One of Allston's finest works, painted during his last year in Europe, the picture contains a dramatic and emotionally charged landscape, a sparse and craggy land overshadowed by masses of gray clouds. This harsh and intense interpretation of nature, dominating man, offers a wholly new vision of nature and of the role of the artist as a creator rather than recorder. The painting, a gift, was the Boston Museum's first registered acquisition.

Collections:
Henry Labouchere (later Lord Taunton), London, before 1828; Mrs. Samuel Hooper and Miss Alice Hooper, Boston.
Museum of Fine Arts, Boston. Gift of Mrs. Samuel Hooper and Miss Alice Hooper, 1870.

Exhibitions:
Washington, D.C., Corcoran Gallery, *The American Muse,* 1959, no. 60, repr.; New York, Metropolitan Museum, *19th-Century America: Paintings and Sculpture,* 1970, no. 6.
Bibliography:
E. P. Richardson, *Allston,* Chicago, 1948, pp. 117, 119–120, 204, pl. XLII.

HENRY SARGENT (1770–1845)
Sargent, who was born in Gloucester, Mass., moved to Boston at nine and was later headed for a mercantile career. After service as an officer in the Revolution, he chose to paint and worked under West in London from 1793 to 1799. In Boston again, his work showed less the influence of the Neoclassicists than the late eighteenth century English painters of portraits and conversation pieces. Although an accomplished painter of portraits and large historical and religious pictures, Sargent is most of interest for his early and exceptional genre paintings.

27
The Dinner Party
Oil on canvas. $59^1/_2$ x 48 inches.
Painted about 1821.
Supposedly represented is a meeting of the Wednesday Evening Club, an informal group of the artist's social and intellectual friends, in the dining room of his house at 10 Franklin Place, then a fashionable district of Boston. A document of well-to-do social life and fashion in Federal Boston, the painting is one of the earliest examples of American genre. Encouraged by its popularity, Sargent painted *The Tea Party* (Boston Museum) a few years later, in which the furnishings are in the latest Empire fashion, rather than Hepplewhite and Sheraton.

Collections:
D. L. Brown, Boston, 1821; Winthrop Henry Sargent, the artist's grandson, Boston; Mrs. Winthrop Sargent, Boston; Mrs. Horatio A. Lamb, her sister, Milton, Mass.
Museum of Fine Arts, Boston. Gift of Mrs. Horatio A. Lamb in memory of Mr. and Mrs. Winthrop Sargent, 1919.

Exhibitions:
Washington, D.C., Corcoran Gallery, *The American Muse,* 1959, no. 103; New York,

25 ALLSTON. Moonlit Landscape

26 ALLSTON. Elijah in the Desert

27 SARGENT. The Dinner Party

28 SULLY. The Torn Hat

Metropolitan Museum, *19th-Century America: Paintings and Sculpture*, 1970, no. 27, repr.

Bibliography:
E. P. Richardson, *American Romantic Painting*, New York, 1945, no. 2, repr.

THOMAS SULLY (1783–1872)

Brought from England as a youth, Sully grew up in Charleston, S.C. After training as a miniaturist with his brother, a brother-in-law and a classmate, Charles Fraser, he worked in Norfolk and Richmond, Va. from 1801 to 1805. He then moved to New York and two years later visited Hartford and Boston, where Gilbert Stuart offered helpful advice; then settled in Philadelphia in 1808. During a year in England from 1809 to 1810, he visited the elderly West but was profoundly influenced by the sleek portrait style of Sir Thomas Lawrence. On returning to Philadelphia he soon replaced Charles Willson Peale as the leading portrait painter of the city, where his elegant and polished style became the vogue of the generation.

28
The Torn Hat

Oil on panel. 19 x 14$\frac{1}{2}$ inches.
Signed and dated on the hatband:
TS 1820 (initials in monogram).
Contrary to his sometimes idealized and impersonal portraits, especially of women, the spontaneous freshness of this painting, one of the most famous in American art, shows Sully at his best. The subject is his son, Thomas Wilcocks Sully (1811–1847), later a portrait painter himself. Sully has treated the subject as genre, and despite a winsome and almost raffish quality, avoids sentimentality.

Collections:
J. Hubbard, Boston, by 1827; Miss Margaret Greene, Boston, 1894.
Museum of Fine Arts, Boston. Gift of Belle Greene and Henry Copley Greene in memory of their mother, Mary Abby Greene, 1916.

Exhibitions:
Philadelphia, Pennsylvania Academy, *Sully Memorial*, 1922, no. 86, repr.; Minneapolis Institute, *Four Centuries of American Art*, 1963–1964.

Bibliography:
E. Biddle and M. Fielding, *Sully*, Philadelphia, 1921, p. 292, no. 1745.

CHESTER HARDING (1792–1866)

Harding, born in Conway, N.H., was raised on farms there and in western New York State. First a house and sign painter, some elementary guidance from an itinerant artist led him into that profession. Although uneducated and untrained, his talent and geniality let to success on painting trips through Ohio, Missouri, Kentucky and New England. In 1822 he sought out Stuart's guidance in Boston. Continued success made possible a trip to London the next year, where he prospered under the influence of Sir Thomas Lawrence. He settled in Boston on his return in 1826, and became one of the most active portraitists in the Northeast.

29
Mrs. Thomas Brewster Coolidge

Oil on canvas. 36$\frac{1}{4}$ x 28 inches.
Painted about 1828–1830.
Harding's portrait of Clarissa Baldwin Coolidge, a clearly fashionable Boston lady, reveals his special skills in rendering the textures and detail of her feathered finery. Despite his training in the elegant portrait style of Lawrence, Harding rarely sought to flatter the features of his subjects.

Collections:
Benjamin Coolidge, Boston; Baldwin Coolidge, Boston; Frank Bulkeley Smith, sold American Association, New York, April 22–23, 1920, no. 147.
The Metropolitan Museum of Art, New York. Rogers Fund, 1920.

Exhibitions:
New York, National Academy of Design, *The American Tradition*, 1951, no. 60; New York, Metropolitan Museum, *19th-Century America: Paintings and Sculpture*, 1970, no. 36, repr.

JOHN WESLEY JARVIS (1780–1840)

Jarvis was brought to Philadelphia from England as a child. From 1796 to 1801, he was apprenticed to the important engraver, Edward Savage. He turned to painting and, charming and gregarious as well, he was by 1814 one of the finest and most active American portraitists, capable of a polished assurance of brushwork and a skill at capturing the character and vitality of his subject. However, a paralytic stroke ended his career and he died destitute.

30
General Andrew Jackson

Oil on canvas. 48$\frac{1}{2}$ x 36 inches.
Painted about 1819.
The illustrious Jackson (1767–1845), former member of the House of Representatives, United States Senator, a Major General in the army, first Governor of Florida, hero of the War of 1812 and destined to become seventh President of the United States, was man of the hour on his New York visit in 1819. An ideal subject for Jarvis' brush, of the many portraits of Jackson made at the time, Jarvis' was acclaimed the best.

Collections:
Samuel Swartwout (?), New York; Manhattan Club.

29 HARDING. Mrs. Thomas Brewster Coolidge

30 JARVIS. General Andrew Jackson

31 HEALY. Euphemia White Van Rensselaer

The Metropolitan Museum of Art, New York.
Harris Brisbane Dick Fund, 1964.

Bibliography:

H. E. Dickson, *John Wesley Jarvis*, New York, 1949, p. 214 f.

GEORGE PETER ALEXANDER HEALY (1813–1894)

Although the son of a poor Boston ship's captain, much of Healy's prolific career as a portrait painter was spent in the cosmopolitan circles of Paris and London. In 1834, several commissions in Boston provided funds for European study. Healy spent a year under the Neoclassic painter Baron Gros, then met Thomas Couture. By his return to America eight years later he had become a highly fashionable portraitist to nobility and society in Paris and London. From 1844 to 1867 he worked primarily in Washington and Chicago, but then lived in Paris again until 1892, traveling regularly to important centers of both continents.

31
Euphemia White Van Rensselaer

Oil on canvas. 45³/₄ x 35¹/₄ inches. Signed and dated lower right: *G. P. A. Healy Paris 1842.*

Euphemia Van Rensselaer (1816–1888) was of one of the most prominent New York State families, extensive land-owners in the Albany area since the days of Dutch rule. Her father Stephen, a major figure in state politics, a General in the War of 1812 and President of the Erie Canal Commission, had also found-ed Rensselaer Polytechnic Institute. Euphemia, the wife of John Church Cruger, was painted in Paris, gracefully posed in a manner reminiscent of Ingres, before an indistinct landscape, probably the Roman Campagna.

Collections:
The family of John Church Cruger, the sub-ject's husband.
The Metropolitan Museum of Art, New York. Bequest of Cornelia Cruger, 1923.

Exhibition:
New York, Metropolitan Museum, *19th-Century America: Paintings and Sculpture*, 1970, no. 68, repr.

Bibliography:
M. De Mare, *G. P. A. Healy*, New York, 1954, p. 109.

THOMAS COLE (1801–1848)

Although English by birth, Cole was founder and guiding force of the Amer-ican Hudson River School of landscape painters. Settled in Ohio with his family, he had resolved by 1820 to be a painter, and was in Philadelphia from 1823 to 1825, strongly interested in Thomas Doughty's landscapes. Moving to New York that year, his own landscapes quickly found influential buyers. His painting trips up the Hudson Valley sketching directly from nature led other artists to follow, and he settled in Cats-kill, N.Y. In 1829 he began a three year trip to England, France, and Italy where his romantic nature was drawn to the art of Claude Lorrain and Turner. In America again, he devoted himself to working in the Catskills, painting land-scapes which infused nature with emo-tional vitality.

32
Expulsion from the Garden of Eden

Oil on canvas. 39 x 54 inches. Signed lower left: *T Cole.* Painted about 1827–1828.

This painting and an unlocated com-panion of the *Garden of Eden* were among his first combining landscape with Biblical history, and anticipate his allegorical series, *The Course of Empire*

and *The Voyage of Life*. He wrote his patron Robert Gilmor that in the pair he was attempting "a higher style of land-scape" than before: in the one giving a "glimpse of the Garden of Eden in its tranquillity," and in the *Expulsion,* "the more terrible objects of nature."

Collections:
Dr. David Hosack, New York; Dr. J. Kearny Rodgers, New York, 1848; James Lenox, New York, 1849; Lenox Library, New York, 1870; Lenox Foundation, New York Public Library, 1895; sold Parke-Bernet Galleries, New York, April 14–16, 1943, no. 533.
Museum of Fine Arts, Boston. M. and M. Karolik Collection, 1947.

Exhibitions:
Rochester, N.Y., University of Rochester Art Gallery, Utica, N.Y., Munson-Williams-Proctor Institute, Albany Institute, and New York, Whitney Museum, *Thomas Cole*, 1969, p. 25, no. 15, repr.

Bibliography:
Boston, MFA, *Karolik Collection of American Paintings*, Cambridge, Mass., 1949, pp. 192–195, no. 89, repr. p. 193.

THOMAS COLE
33
A View Near Tivoli (Morning)

Oil on canvas. 13³/₄ x 23¹/₈ inches. Signed and dated on the back: *T. Cole/ Florence/1832.*

After wintering in Florence, Cole spent the spring of 1832 in Rome, occupying the studio of Claude Lorrain, filling his eyes and spirit with the wonders of an-cient Rome. He was attracted even more by the spreading beauty of the Campagna with its fragments of history settling into the landscape. On return-ing to Florence that summer, he painted a number of outstanding works, this among them, which vividly captured the loveliness and transient atmosphere of the area.

32 COLE. Expulsion from the Garden of Eden

33 COLE. A View Near Tivoli (Morning)

Collections:
Gift of the artist to William A. Adams, 1834;
Henry G. Marquand, New York, by 1893;
sold American Art Association, New York,
Jan. 23, 1903, no. 81 (as *A Roman Aqueduct*);
Samuel P. Avery, Jr., 1903.
The Metropolitan Museum of Art, New York.
Rogers Fund, 1903.
Exhibitions:
New York, National Academy of Design,
1833, no. 51; Rochester, N.Y., University of
Rochester Art Gallery, Utica, N.Y., Munson-
Williams-Proctor Institute, Albany Institute,
and New York, Whitney Museum, *Thomas
Cole*, 1969, p. 28, no. 23, repr. p. 52.

SAMUEL F. B. MORSE (1791–1872)

Samuel Finley Breese Morse, a minis-
ter's son, was born in Charlestown,
Mass. and on graduation from Yale
determined, over his father's objec-
tions, to be an artist. He studied with
West and Allston in London from 1811
to 1815. Despite aspirations to be a historical painter, on returning to America
he was forced to work as an itinerant
artist for several years. In 1823 he
settled in New York and three years
later was founder and first President of
the National Academy of Design, established in opposition to the lethargic
American Academy dominated by John
Trumbull. The Lafayette portrait commission of 1825 (City Hall, New York),
confirmed his artistic excellence, but
professional and personal tragedies,
and persistant financial problems, increasingly focussed his efforts on his inventions. After 1837 he abandoned
painting to perfect his invention of the
telegraph (and the Morse Code).

34
The Muse – Susan Walker Morse
Oil on canvas. 73³/₄ x 57⁵/₈ inches.
Painted between 1835 and 1837.

The portrait of Morse's daughter Susan
(1819–1885), his last major painting, is
a monumental achievement, almost in
the grand manner of history painting, a
rich and elegant yet sympathetic portrayal of maidenly virtue. The dramatic
setting and idealized rendering, totally
out of keeping with his own financial
plight, form a bridge between the Neoclassic tradition and the Romantic tenor
of the Victorian period.

Collections:
The family of the subject; Herbert Lee Pratt,
New York.
The Metropolitan Museum of Art, New York.
Bequest of Herbert L. Pratt, 1945.
Exhibitions:
New York, Metropolitan Museum, *Samuel
F. B. Morse*, 1932, p. 40; New York, Metro-
poltian Museum, *19th-Century America:
Paintings and Sculpture*, 1970, no. 31, repr.

ASHER B. DURAND (1796–1886)

Asher Brown Durand, born in Jefferson
Village (now Maplewood), N. J., and
later a leader of the first generation of
the Hudson River School, was at forty
the foremost engraver in America. Lu-
man Reed, the New York collector, encouraged him to abandon engraving for
painting about 1836. Like his close
friend, Thomas Cole, Durand made
painting excursions along the Hudson
and in the mountains of upstate New
York and New England. Another collector, Jonathan Sturges, helped provide a
trip to Europe in 1840 and 1841 where
the paintings of Claude Lorrain, seen in
Paris and Italy, profoundly affected his
work. He combined the engraver's pre-
cision and a lyric mood and lighting
from Claude to produce idyllic landscapes, romantically idealizing counterparts to the poetry of Wordsworth and
William Cullen Bryant.

35
In the Woods
Oil on canvas. 60³/₄ x 48 inches.
Signed and dated lower right: *A. B.
Durand/1855*.
In the Woods, celebrated at the time as
one of Durand's finest works, is one of
a series of sylvan views that resulted
from a commission by his patron, Jonathan Sturges. Painted in the studio, after
sketches from nature, this monumental
painting captures not the usual spreading vista, but the quiet spirit and
beauty of a secluded glen.

Collections:
The Sturges family.
The Metropolitan Museum of Art, New York.
Gift in memory of Jonathan Sturges by his
children, 1895.
Exhibition:
Baltimore Museum of Art, *Romanticism in
America*, 1940.
Bibliography:
J. Durand, *The Life and Times of Asher B.
Durand*, New York, 1894, p. 175.

FREDERICK E. CHURCH (1826–1900)

Frederick Edwin Church, born in Hartford, Conn., received some training
there, and in 1844 became a pupil and
friend of Thomas Cole, living in the
house at Catskill, N.Y. He settled in
New York in 1848, following Cole's
death, but regularly visited the Hudson
Valley, and coastal and inland New England. Visits to the mountains of Colum-
bia and Ecuador in 1853 and 1857 provided some of his grandest and most
romantic subjects. From 1867 to 1869
he made an extensive tour of Europe
and the Near East as far as Greece, Jeru-
salem, and Damascus, which also became subjects of major works. In 1872
Church constructed his fabulous home,
Olana, but five years later was stricken

34 MORSE. The Muse – Susan Walker Morse

35 DURAND. In the Woods

36 CHURCH. The Parthenon

37 CROPSEY. Mt. Chocorua, New Hampshire, Autumn

38 KENSETT. Lake George

with rheumatism which soon ended his painting career.

36
The Parthenon
Oil on canvas. 44$\frac{1}{4}$ x 72$\frac{1}{8}$ inches. Signed and dated lower left: *F. E. Church/1871*.
On his visit to Athens in April of 1869, Church made several sketch drawings (Cooper Union, New York) of the Parthenon. From those visual notes he created this vivid depiction of that great architectural monument surrounded by the scattered fragments of the past glory of the Acropolis. Unlike his almost melodramatic fantasies of natural wonders – mountains, gorges and spuming waterfalls – *The Parthenon* is presented with a mood of timeless repose.

Collection:
Commissioned by Morris K. Jesup, New York. The Metropolitan Museum of Art, New York. Bequest of Maria DeWitt Jesup, 1915.
Exhibitions:
Paris, *Exposition Universelle*, 1878, no. 21; Los Angeles County Museum of Art and San Francisco, De Young Memorial Museum, *American Paintings from The Metropolitan Museum*, 1966, p. 82, no. 48, repr. color.
Bibliography:
J. T. Flexner, *That Wilder Image*, New York, 1962, p. 166; D. C. Huntington, *The Landscapes of Frederick Edwin Church*, New York, 1966, pp. 96, 104, 107, 119.

JASPER FRANCIS CROPSEY
(1823–1900)
Cropsey, a native born New Yorker, trained as an architect yet became one of the foremost members of the Hudson River School of landscape painters. Already an exceptional artist in his early twenties, he made an extensive tour of Europe from 1847 to 1849. In Rome he occupied the studio once used by Cole, an artist who emphatically influenced him at the outset of his career. On returning to America he worked in the Hudson Valley, New England and Pennsylvania summers, and in winter expanded his studies into more formal compositions. In England again from 1857 to 1863, he then settled in Hastings-on-Hudson and produced numbers of landscapes, usually autumn scenes.

37
Mt. Chocorua, New Hampshire, Autumn
Oil on canvas. 28$\frac{1}{2}$ x 35$\frac{1}{2}$ inches. Signed lower left: *J. F. Cropsey*. Painted in the early 1870's.
This richly colored panoramic view of Mt. Chocorua, one of the most popular subjects among the Hudson River painters, is one of the finest of Cropsey's later works. The more overtly dramatic mood of his early landscapes, under the influence of Allston and Cole, has given way here to a more placid and detailed eulogy of the American landscape in its bright autumn aspect.

Collection:
John Lenz.
The Metropolitan Museum of Art, New York. Bertram F. and Susie Brummer Foundation, Inc., Gift, 1961.
Exhibition:
Manchester, N. H., Currier Gallery, *Artists in the White Mountains*, 1955, no. 8.

JOHN FREDERICK KENSETT
(1816–1872)
Kensett was born in Cheshire, Conn., the son of an emigrant British engraver, and became an engraver himself in New Haven, New York and Albany. Partly influenced by the engraver-painter Asher Durand, John Casilaer and others, he turned to landscape painting, and in 1840 joined them on an extended trip to Europe. First in the English countryside, but especially in and about Paris and Rome, Kensett concentratedly sketched from nature. In 1847 he settled in New York, but traveled regularly to upper New York and New England and along the New England coast. During succeeding years, which included visits to Europe and the American West, he became one of the most successful of the second generation of Hudson River School painters. Prominent in official American art circles, he was a founder and trustee of the Metropolitan Museum.

38
Lake George
Oil on canvas. 44 x 66$\frac{1}{4}$ inches. Signed and dated lower right: *J. F.* (in monogram) *K. 1869*.
This, one of Kensett's finest paintings, was done near the end of his life. In monumental scope and subtly controlled detailed it captures the quiet grandeur of nature. Seen through moist summer atmosphere, the rippled surface of the lake surrounded by the softly textured mountains are full testimony to his mastery.

Collection:
Commissioned by Morris K. Jesup, New York. The Metropolitan Museum of Art, New York. Bequest of Maria DeWitt Jesup, 1915.
Exhibitions:
American Federation of Arts, New York (circulating exhibition), *Kensett*, 1968–1969, no. 40, repr. (shown New York, Whitney Museum only); New York, Metropolitan Museum, *19th-Century America: Paintings and Sculpture*, 1970, no. 124, repr.

39 GIFFORD. Kauterskill Falls

40 FIELD. Joseph Moore and His Family

SANFORD ROBINSON GIFFORD (1823–1880)

Gifford was born in Greenfield, N.Y. and received brief training in New York about 1845. A painting tour of the Catskills and Berkshires the next year focussed his interest on landscape. The years 1855 to 1858 he devoted to study in England and especially Italy where he was fascinated by Turner's atmospheric effects in painting and by the misty atmosphere of the Roman Campagna. Gifford was a leading member of the Luminists, who shared an interest in the effects of light and atmosphere on landscape. He later made a second trip to Europe, also extensively visited the American West, but mainly worked in New York and the mountains of the Northeast.

39
Kauterskill Falls

Oil on canvas. 48 x 39$^7/_8$ inches.
Signed and dated lower left: *S. R. Gifford/1862.*

Perhaps more than any artist of his time, Gifford concentrated upon the luminous effects of light and atmosphere on landscape. In some respects comparable to French Impressionism, he subtly dissolved the forms of landscape, crisply flickering with color, behind a translucent veil of atmosphere.

Collection:
Morris K. Jesup, New York.
The Metropolitan Museum of Art, New York. Bequest of Maria DeWitt Jesup, 1915.
Exhibitions:
New York, Metropolitan Museum, *The Taste of the Seventies*, 1946, no.111 (listed as *Kaaterskill Clove*); New York, Metropolitan Museum, *19th-Century America: Paintings and Sculpture*, 1970, no.101, repr.
Bibliography:
J. T. Flexner, *That Wilder Image*, Boston and Toronto, 1962, p. 283, repr. p. 285.

ERASTUS SALISBURY FIELD (1805–1900)

Field, an itinerant primitive portrait painter, lived most of his life in the vicinity of Leverett, his birthplace in Western Massachusetts. Despite a few months in Morse's New York studio in 1824, he was essentially self-taught. In fact he seems to have consciously preferred the decorative primitive style which he retained although again exposed to the major art currents of New York from 1841 to 1848. He worked primarily in rural Massachusetts and Connecticut, rarely signed his paintings and, until relatively recently remained unrecognized despite an individual style of detailed, richly patterned and colored likenesses. After his wife's death in 1859 he concentrated on highly imaginative and vividly colored interpretations of Biblical subjects.

40
Joseph Moore and His Family

Oil on canvas. 82$^3/_4$ x 93$^1/_4$ inches.
Painted in 1839.

Field's portrait masterpiece formally poses Joseph Moore (1804–1855), a hatter and itinerant dentist, his wife Almira, two of their children (on the right) and two children of Mrs. Moore's late sister, in their Ware, Mass. parlor. Field has transformed the simple setting into a richly complex visual feast. The monumental figures, dressed severely in black and white, are almost abstractly composed before a highly decorative background. The brightly patterned painted carpet, shuttered windows and furnishings all accentuate the quiet strength of the figures and heighten the painting's vitality.

Collection:
Helen E. Farrar, great-granddaughter of Joseph Moore, Sherborn, Mass.

Museum of Fine Arts, Boston. M. and M. Karolik Collection, 1958.
Exhibitions:
Brussels, World's Fair, *Universal and International Exhibition*, 1958, no. 81; Williamsburg, Va., Abby Aldrich Rockefeller Folk Art Collection, *Field*, 1963, no. 76.
Bibliography:
T. N. Maytham, "Two Faces of New England Portrait Painting," *Boston MFA Bulletin*, 1963, LXI, no. 323, pp. 31–38, fig.1.

ANONYMOUS, Nineteenth Century
41
Meditation by the Sea

Oil on canvas. 13$^1/_2$ x 19$^1/_2$ inches.
Painted about 1850–1860.

This extraordinary painting by a mid-century hand from whom no other works are known, demonstrates the esthetic heights attainable by the folk or primitive artist. The absence of ordinary technical knowledge only serves to enhance the mood and vitality of the painting, allowing the artist's individuality to seek its own expression. The rhythmically patterned waves stimulate the sense of movement, while the minute but finely drawn figure silently contemplates their roll before an endless stretch of beach and the clean sweep of sea and sky. Instead of traditional technique, the painting offers us a highly sophisticated taste and the universal response of man to nature.

Collection:
Maxim Karolik, Newport, R.I.
Museum of Fine Arts, Boston. M. and M. Karolik Collection, 1945.
Exhibitions:
New York, Museum of Modern Art, *Romantic Painting in America*, 1943, no. 213; London, Tate Gallery, *American Painting*, 1946, no.4.
Bibliography:
Boston, MFA, *Karolik Collection of American Paintings*, Cambridge, Mass., 1949, p. 52,

41 ANONYMOUS. Meditation by the Sea

repr. p. 53; J. Wilmerding, *A History of American Marine Painting*, Boston, 1968, p. 38, fig. 25.

GEORGE CALEB BINGHAM
(1811–1879)

Bingham, born in Augusta County, Va. as a child migrated with his family to the Missouri frontier. He was raised as a farmer and artisan, but a chance meeting with Chester Harding turned his interest to painting. He studied briefly at the Pennsylvania Academy in Philadelphia in 1838, then spent the next six years, primarily as a portraitist, in Philadelphia, Washington, and New York. Except for frequent trips East, Bingham lived in Missouri after 1844, working almost exclusively on his now universally admired genre scenes of river and city life on the frontier; his exuberant paintings of political life are among his best. The most important genre artist of Western America, his work is distinguished by special clarity of form and luminous atmosphere.

42
Wood-Boatmen on a River

Oil on canvas. 29 x 36 inches.
Signed and dated lower left: *G. C. Bingham/1854.*

Bingham's views of the life of the rivermen, the most famous and characteristic aspect of his œuvre, are filled with a broad diversity of themes and spirit, ranging from the gay revels of the *Jolly Flatboatmen* to the lyrical quietude of this painting. Although possibly painted in Philadelphia where Bingham worked during much of 1854, the work is a poetic and profound expression of peaceful simplicity. Bingham's night scenes are among the rarest and most beautiful examples of his work.

Collections:

Col. J. L. D. Morrison, St. Louis; Charles Holmes, about 1865; Alfred Clifford, about 1885; Oliver M. Clifford, 1927; with Max Safron, New York, 1944; Mr. and Mrs. Maxim Karolik, Newport, R. I., 1945.
Museum of Fine Arts, Boston. M. and M. Karolik Collection, 1946.

Exhibition:

Washington, National Collection of Fine Arts, Cleveland Museum, University of California at Los Angeles, Art Galleries, *Bingham*, 1967–1968, p. 21, no. 27, fig. 20.

Bibliography:

Boston, MFA, *Karolik Collection of American Paintings*, Cambridge, Mass., 1949, pp. 108, 110, no. 55, repr. p. 109; J. F. McDermott, *George Caleb Bingham, River Portraitist*, Norman, Okla., 1959, pp. 114, 418, no. 82, repr. pl. 48; E. M. Bloch, *Bingham, Evolution of an Artist; Bingham: A Catalogue Raisonné*, Berkeley and Los Angeles, 1967, I, pp. 107–110, 112, pls. 70, 74; II, p. 92, no. 234.

FITZ HUGH LANE (1804–1865)

Lane was born in Gloucester, Mass., and retained a deep affinity for the look and life of coastal New England. Crippled by infantile paralysis, he first worked, about 1832, in Pendleton's lithography shop in Boston, then with another Boston publisher and finally set up his own lithography business. In 1848 he returned permanently to Gloucester, except for brief trips to Maine, New York, Baltimore and Puerto Rico. Although a popular painter in his day, he remained virtually unknown to modern audiences until the 1940's, and is now one of the most widely admired of the nineteenth century American marine painters.

43
Boston Harbor

Oil on canvas. 26 1/4 x 42 inches.
Painted about 1850–1855.

One of several versions of the subject, the detailed description of ships and their rigging reveals Lane's intimate knowledge of a major mid-century harbor. Above all, the painting displays those special qualities of light and atmosphere unique to his work, which associate him with the Luminist group that included Martin Johnson Heade and Sanford Gifford.

Collections:

Probably Mrs. Charles M. Peirce, New Bedford, Mass.; Mrs. Willis E. Lougee, her daughter, New Bedford; Mrs. Grace H. Sargeant, her daughter, New Bedford; Mrs. Thomas W. Farnsworth, Jr., her daughter, New Bedford, about 1960.
Museum of Fine Arts, Boston. M. and M. Karolik Collection by exchange and gift of John Wilmerding, 1966.

Exhibition:

Boston, MFA, *Centennial Acquisitions: Art Treasures for Tomorrow*, 1970, p. 120, no. 84, repr. color.

Bibliography:

J. Wilmerding, *A History of American Marine Painting*, Boston, 1968, p. 162, pl. XIII.

WILLIAM SIDNEY MOUNT
(1807–1868)

Mount, born in Setauket, L. I. and brought up in nearby Stony Brook, maintained a lifelong attachment to the area. First apprenticed to his sign painter brother in New York, he was then a pupil at the National Academy of Design when it opened in 1826. Although he painted portraits throughout his career, his genre paintings of country life constitute his great contribution to American painting. In 1837 he settled in Stony Brook and continued to produce unpretentious yet fresh, realistic and universally appealing views of rural life. Like Bingham in the West, Mount carried the nineteenth-century genre tradition to its highest point.

42 BINGHAM. Wood-Boatmen on a River

43 LANE. Boston Harbor

44 MOUNT. The Bone Player

45 MOUNT. Cider Making

46 THOMPSON. A "Pic Nick", Camden, Maine

44

The Bone Player

Oil on canvas. 36 x 29 inches.
Signed and dated lower right: *Wm. S. Mount 1856.*

One of Mount's many Negro subjects, the painting is from a group of four studies of large single figures with musical instruments and pair to *The Banjo Player* (Suffolk Museum and Carriage House, Stony Brook, L. I.). These striking single-figure genre subjects are unusual in his work for their relative isolation of the subject from a specific setting. Contrary to many nineteenth century American artists, Mount neither lampooned nor sentimentalized the Negro.

Collections:
John D. Jones, 1858; Mrs. Edward Floyd-Jones, New York; Maxim Karolik, Newport, R. I.
Museum of Fine Arts, Boston. M. and M. Karolik Collection, 1948.

Exhibition:
Washington, National Gallery, St. Louis, City Art Museum, New York, Whitney Museum, and San Francisco, De Young Museum, *Painter of Rural America: William Sidney Mount*, 1968–1969, no. 38, repr. p. 57.

Bibliography:
Boston, MFA, *Karolik Collection of American Paintings*, Cambridge, Mass., 1949, p. 438, repr. p. 439.

WILLIAM SIDNEY MOUNT

45

Cider Making

Oil on canvas. 27 x 34 1/8 inches.
Signed and dated lower left: *Wm. S. Mount./1841.*
Cider Making, one of Mount's finest paintings, characterizes the significance of genre painting in American art. In the clear light of early autumn, he has depicted a truly American scene, unaffectedly capturing real people at work

and at play in a real place. His is an instantly appealing democratic art form which while nostalgic, avoids the romantic idealization of the Hudson River landscape style and the formal flattery of portraiture.

Collections:
Commissioned by Charles Augustus Davis, New York; William J. Smith, by 1897; Ida L. Hume, 1931; Edwin Hume, her son, 1937.
The Metropolitan Museum of Art, New York. Charles Allen Munn Bequest, 1966.

Exhibitions:
Washington, National Gallery, St. Louis, City Art Museum, New York, Whitney Museum, and San Francisco, De Young Museum, *Painter of Rural America: William Sidney Mount*, 1968–1969, p. 31, no. 19, repr. color p. 30; New York, Metropolitan Museum, *19th-Century America: Paintings and Sculpture*, 1970, no. 53, repr.

Bibliography:
S. P. Feld, "In the Midst of 'High Vintage'," *Metropolitan Museum Bulletin*, April, 1967, pp. 292–307, repr. color.

JEROME B. THOMPSON (1814–1886)

One of the lesser known but increasingly admired nineteenth century genre painters, Thompson was born in Middleboro, Mass., the son of Cephas Thompson, the portrait painter. He first worked in Barnstable on Cape Cod as a sign and ornamental painter, but also did some portraits. In 1835, he opened a studio in New York and became successful with his rural genre pictures. A trip to England in 1852 introduced him to the art of the English Victorian painters whose broader treatment and large scale he absorbed into his own style. On returning several years later, he settled in Mineola, L. I. where he established a successful experimental farm, and later developed another farm in Glen Gardner, N. J.

46

A "Pic Nick," Camden, Maine

Oil on canvas. 41 x 62 inches.
Painted about 1850.
This charming glimpse of rural American social life is perhaps Thompson's finest painting. For years this extraordinary picture was attributed to Jeremiah P. Hardy, a New England painter of portraits and more sentimental genre scenes. Despite significant stylistic differences, Thompson's approach and content are similar to those of Mount, a fellow resident of Long Island, whose paintings at least he must have known.

Collections:
Found in Red Bank, N.J.; Maxim Karolik, Newport, R. I.
Museum of Fine Arts, Boston. M. and M. Karolik Collection, 1946.

Bibliography:
B N. Parker, "A 'Pic Nick,' Camden, Maine, by Jerome B. Thompson," *Boston MFA Bulletin*, 1952, no. 282, pp. 79–82, repr.

MARTIN JOHNSON HEADE (1819–1904)

Heade was born in Lumberville (Bucks Co.), Pa. As a youth he showed a talent for art and was sent to the Quaker primitive, Edward Hicks, but also received training from the nephew, a genre painter Thomas Hicks. He was in Rome from 1838 to 1840, was principally in New York during the forties but also roamed the East doing portraits and genre paintings. After another more productive Roman trip and work in the Midwest, Heade lived on the eastern seaboard from 1855 to 1885 concentrating on landscape, especially his luminously atmospheric marshland scenes. Also a naturalist, he made several trips to Central and South America in the 1860's, producing numerous

47 HEADE. Approaching Storm: Beach Near Newport

48 ROESEN. Still Life: Flowers

paintings of hummingbirds and exotic flowers, for an ultimately unrealized lithographic portfolio on the subject. In 1885 he settled in St. Augustine, Fla. and continued to paint marsh scenes and bird and flower pictures.

47
Approaching Storm:
Beach Near Newport
Oil on canvas. 28 x 58 1/4 inches.
Painted about 1867.
This masterpiece displays the more moodily romantic nature of Heade's art that sets him apart from the majority of Hudson River painters. In his landscapes he constantly emphasized the transient spirit or atmosphere of his subject: the looming threat of storm, the dappled passage of clouds over the saturated air of a still marsh, burning sunsets or the haunting silhouette of haystacks at nightfall.

Collections:
Henry Goddard Pickering, Boston, 1926; Mrs. Richard Y. Fitz Gerald, Boston; Stephen C. Clark, New York; Maxim Karolik, Newport, R. I.
Museum of Fine Arts, Boston. M. and M. Karolik Collection, 1945.
Exhibition:
Boston, MFA, College Park, University of Maryland, and New York, Whitney Museum, *Heade*, 1969, no. 27, repr.
Bibliography:
R. G. McIntyre, *Heade*, New York, 1948, p. 45; Boston, MFA, *Karolik Collection of American Paintings*, Cambridge, Mass., 1949, p. 308, repr. p. 309; J. Wilmerding, *A History of American Marine Painting*, Boston, 1968, p. 182, fig. 122.

SEVERIN ROESEN (died about 1871)
Little is known of Roesen's early life except that he was a still life and porcelain and enamel painter in Cologne, Germany who emigrated to America about 1848. He was apparently in New York from about 1850 to 1857 and in Williamsport, Pa. from 1858 to 1870. He reputedly died in a Philadelphia almshouse in 1871.

48
Still Life: Flowers
Oil on canvas. 40 x 50 3/8 inches.
Our real records of Roesen lie in his many meticulously painted and elaborately composed still life paintings of fruit and flowers. Brightly colored, almost brittle in their crispness, his paintings clearly derive from the porcelain decorator's craft and repertoire. Of the many American practitioners of this type of still life painting, Roesen is surely the finest.

Collection:
The Metropolitan Museum of Art, New York. Charles Allen Munn Bequest; Fosburgh Fund, Inc., Gift; Mr. and Mrs. J. William Middendorf II Gift; and Henry G. Keasbey Bequest, 1967.
Exhibition:
New York, Metropolitan Museum, *19th-Century America: Paintings and Sculpture*, 1970, no. 104, repr.

EASTMAN JOHNSON (1824–1906)
Johnson was born in Lovell, Maine, and at sixteen was an apprentice in Bufford's lithography shop in Boston. Within a year he took up portrait drawing and was an active itinerant artist in New England and in Washington, until 1849. He began to work in oil and trained for five years under Emmanuel Leutze at the Düsseldorf Academy.

During the next four extremely successful years in The Hague and in Paris, he expanded his interest in genre painting. Johnson returned to America in 1855 and settled in New York in 1859. He concentrated on genre painting in the sixties and seventies, developing a freer and more expressive style than the more muted discipline of the Düsseldorf tradition. After 1880, portrait commissions dominated his interests.

49
Corn Husking at Nantucket
Oil on canvas. 27 5/8 x 54 1/2 inches.
Signed lower right: *E. Johnson*. Painted about 1875.
Johnson first frequented Nantucket in the early 1870's. That secluded area, and his recollections of rural life in his native Maine, were the sources for his best genre paintings. This picture, the final sketch for the more finished version in the Art Institute of Chicago, captures with glowing vitality the charming interplay of ages and personalities at this traditional rural social event.

Collection:
Estate of the artist; sold American Art Association, New York, Feb. 26–27, 1907, no. 146.
The Metropolitan Museum of Art, New York. Rogers Fund, 1907.
Exhibitions:
New York, Metropolitan Museum, *Life in America*, 1939, no. 233; Brooklyn Museum, *An American Genre Painter, Eastman Johnson*, 1940, no. 54.
Bibliography:
E. U. Crosby, *Eastman Johnson at Nantucket*, Nantucket, Mass., 1944, p. 12, no. C 2.

49 JOHNSON. Corn Husking at Nantucket

50 BIERSTADT. View from the Wind River Mountains, Wyoming

51 BIERSTADT. The Buffalo Trail

ALBERT BIERSTADT (1830–1902)

Bierstadt was brought as an infant from his native Solingen, Germany to New Bedford, Mass. He returned in 1853 to study painting at the flourishing Düsseldorf Academy and also toured Germany, Switzerland and Italy until 1857. He then established himself in New York, but the next year joined the Lander expedition through the American West. That trip and another in 1863 through Colorado to California provided the inspiration and substance for the rest of his career. Uncounted oil sketches taken directly from nature were later developed into often vast canvasses depicting the untouched beauty and grandeur of the West. Except for frequent travels, he lived in Irvington-on-the-Hudson and then New York City for the remainder of his life.

50

View from the Wind River Mountains, Wyoming

Oil on canvas. 30$\frac{1}{4}$ x 48$\frac{1}{4}$ inches.
Signed and dated lower left: *A. Bierstadt 1860* (A and B in monogram). The painting was done during the first winter after Bierstadt's return from the Lander expedition, and characterizes the paintings which launched his success. Bierstadt accentuated the Hudson River School tradition of realistic technique and idealistic interpretation. Here he conveys the vast scale and harmony between man and nature that could exist at that time.

Collections:
John Nelson Borland, Boston; Francis Lee Higginson, Boston; William Gibson Borland, Boston; Maxim Karolik, Newport, R. I.
Museum of Fine Arts, Boston. M. and M. Karolik Collection, 1947.
Bibliography:
Boston, MFA, *Karolik Collection of American Paintings*, Cambridge, Mass., 1949, pp. 82–84, repr. no. 39.

ALBERT BIERSTADT
51
The Buffalo Trail

Oil on canvas. 32 x 48 inches.
Signed lower right: *A Bierstadt* (A and B in monogram). Painted in 1867–1868. One of the most emotionally compelling of Bierstadt's paintings, the silent, endless procession of animals under a stormy sky conveys a special nostalgia for the modern audience. The dramatic lighting and coloration in some respects parallel Bierstadt's vast views of stormy alpine valleys, which also had great popularity during the third quarter of the nineteenth century.

Collections:
At one time owned in England (English label on reverse); Private Collection, N.Y.; sold Parke-Bernet Galleries, New York, Feb. 26–27, 1947, no. 64; Maxim Karolik, Newport, R. I.
Museum of Fine Arts, Boston. M. and M. Karolik Collection, 1947.
Bibliography:
Boston, MFA, *Karolik Collection of American Paintings,* Cambridge, Mass., 1949, pp. 90–92, repr. no. 44.

GEORGE INNESS (1825–1894)

Inness was born in Newburgh, N.Y., and except for a brief period of training under the French landscapist, Régis Gignoux, in New York, he was basically self-taught. By 1845 he had a studio in New York, and in 1847 made the first of several journeys to Europe, that time to England and Italy. From 1859 to 1864, he lived in Medfield, Mass., then in Eaglesswood, N. J and after 1878 in Montclair, N. J. Inness' earlier style was strongly influenced by the *plein-air* approach of the French Barbizon painters, which was later supplanted by influence from Cole and Durand. At first detailed and naturalistic, Inness' paintings became increasingly expressive and atmospheric until, in the 1880's, they became almost completely imaginative and intangible: evocative color harmonies of luminous greens and yellows.

52
Lake Nemi

Oil on canvas. 30 x 45 inches.
Signed and dated lower right: *Inness Nemi 1872.*
This dramatic and vividly colored painting displays Inness' knowledge of the dynamics and atmosphere of Turner's work. It also parallels the magnificent Luminist view of *Lake Nemi* (Toledo Museum of Art) painted by Sanford Gifford fifteen years earlier. Inness wrote to the couple who commissioned the painting: "I trust you will find the picture of Lake Nemi one of my very best, as I intended it should be, and I am happy to say it was so looked upon by all who saw it at my studio." (Albano, 1872).

Collections:
Commissioned by Mr. and Mrs. A. D. Williams, Roxbury, Mass., 1872; Miss Ada Hersey, Roxbury, 1905.
Museum of Fine Arts, Boston. Gift of the Misses Hersey, 1949.
Bibliography:
L. Ireland, *Inness*, Austin, Texas, 1965, no. 560, repr.

GEORGE INNESS
53
Autumn Oaks

Oil on canvas. 21$\frac{1}{8}$ x 30$\frac{1}{4}$ inches.
Signed lower right: *G. Inness.* Painted about 1875.

52 INNESS. Lake Nemi

53 INNESS. Autumn Oaks

This exceptional painting was done in the year following Inness' last trip to France and Italy. Presumably a view of the New Jersey countryside, it incorporates the colors and content of his earlier interest in Barbizon art with the broader and more emotional handling of his later work.

Collection:
George I. Seney, New York.
The Metropolitan Museum of Art, New York. Gift of George I. Seney, 1887.

Exhibition:
Springfield, Mass., George Walter Vincent Smith Museum, Brooklyn Museum, and Montclair, N. J., Art Museum, *Inness*, 1946, no. 25.

Bibliography:
G. Inness, Jr., *Life, Art, and Letters of George Inness,* New York, 1917, pp. 232–233; L. Ireland, *Inness,* Austin, Texas, 1965, p. 179, no. 729, repr.

WINSLOW HOMER (1836–1910)

Homer, one of the greatest of American painters, was born in Boston and grew up in then rural Cambridge. He was apprenticed to the Boston lithographer J. H. Bufford from 1854 to 1857. In 1859 he moved to New York as a freelance illustrator, especially for *Harper's Weekly,* and at the outbreak of the war was a correspondent. His first paintings, about this time, were of daily life behind the lines, not battle itself. A trip to France in 1866–1867 had little impact, and again in New York he began to paint charming, fresh and solidly realistic genre and landscape: young women and children at play or at leisure. Beginning in the 1870's oils and brilliant watercolors capture woodland scenes: hunting, fishing, and life in the mountains. Following a trip to England from 1881 to 1882, Homer became increasingly withdrawn and possessed by the

sea. He moved to Prout's Neck, a fishing village on the Maine coast, and in progressively dark and bold paintings recorded the elemental drama of the sea and man's life on and by it.

54
Snap the Whip
Oil on canvas. 12 x 20 inches.
Signed and dated lower right: *HOMER 1872*
Homer's many paintings of children in school or at play or "just thinking" are among his most delightful contributions to American art and life. Sympathetic yet unsentimental, they capture with vital naturalism the light, air and above all the spirit of his subject. The painting is one of two versions; the other (Butler Institute of American Art, Youngstown, Ohio) has a mountainous background and more figures.

Collection:
Christian A. Zabriskie, New York. The Metropolitan Museum of Art, New York. Gift of Christian A. Zabriskie, 1950.

Exhibitions:
New York, Metropolitan Museum, *19th-Century America: Paintings and Sculpture,* 1970, no. 159, repr.

Bibliography:
L. Goodrich, *Homer,* New York, 1944, pp. 34, 43, 45, 69, 72, 215; A. T. Gardner, *Homer,* New York, 1961, p. 204, repr. p. 146.

WINSLOW HOMER
55
Searchlight, Harbor Entrance, Santiago de Cuba
Oil on canvas. 30¹/₂ x 50¹/₂ inches.
Signed lower right: *W. HOMER.* Painted in 1901.
This powerfully stark night view of a section of Morro Castle in the harbor of Santiago, Cuba is one of Homer's most remarkable pictures. He had made a drawing (Cooper Union collection, New York) of Morro Castle during a

Cuban visit in 1885–1886. His painting, of fifteen years later, was partly prompted by his remembrance of the decisive naval engagement of the Spanish-American war which took place at this harbor in 1898.

Collection:
George A. Hearn, New York.
The Metropolitan Museum of Art, New York. Gift of George A. Hearn, 1906.

Exhibition:
Washington, National Gallery, and New York, Metropolitan Museum, *Homer,* 1958–1959, no. 73, repr. p. 103.

Bibliography:
L. Goodrich, *Homer,* New York, 1944, pp. 90, 172–173, 187; P. C. Beam, *Homer at Prout's Neck,* Boston and Toronto, 1966, pp. 219–220.

WINSLOW HOMER
56
Long Branch, New Jersey
Oil on canvas. 16 x 21³/₄ inches.
Signed and dated lower right: *Winslow Homer/1869.*
This is one of the best known of Homer's early paintings and, although independently conceived, it parallels the *plein-air* approach to nature of his French Impressionist contemporaries. One particularly thinks of Boudin's beach scenes with fashionable young ladies enjoying the sun and sea air.

Collections:
Robert Vonnoh, Philadelphia, before 1906; Sherrill Babcock, New York.
Museum of Fine Arts, Boston. Charles Henry Hayden Fund, 1941.

Exhibitions:
London, Tate Gallery, *American Painting,* 1946, no. 111; Washington, National Gallery, and New York, Metropolitan Museum, *Homer,* 1958–1959, no. 15.

Bibliography:
L. Goodrich, *Homer,* New York, 1944, pp. 41, 51, repr. p. 9; E. P. Richardson, *Painting in America,* New York, 1956, p. 315, fig. 128.

54 HOMER. Snap the Whip
55 HOMER. Searchlight, Harbor Entrance, Santiago de Cuba

56 HOMER. Long Branch, New Jersey

57 HOMER. The Lookout – "All's Well"

WINSLOW HOMER

57

The Lookout – "All's Well"

Oil on canvas. 40 x 30 1/4 inches.
Signed and dated lower right: *Homer/
1896.*

With the passage of years, Homer's
style displayed an increasing breadth of
handling and concern for the dramatic
potentials of pictorial means them-
selves. As with many of his paintings at
Prout's Neck, *The Lookout* embodies
man's relationship with the sea, render-
ed here in monumental, yet suggestive
terms, and painted in a harmony of
nocturnal blues. The eccentric and fragmentary composition – the raised hand
slickered figure, a snatch of sea – may
reflect an awareness of Japanese prints.

Collection:
Thomas B. Clarke, 1897; *Thomas B. Clarke
Collection Sale,* American Art Association,
New York, Feb. 14–17, 1899, no. 84.
Museum of Fine Arts, Boston. William Wil-
kins Warren Fund, 1899.

Exhibitions:
New York, Whitney Museum, *Homer Centenary,* 1936, no. 29; Washington, National
Gallery, and New York, Metropolitan Museum, *Homer,* 1958–1959, no. 68, repr. p. 97;
Bowdoin, Maine, Bowdoin College, *Homer
at Prout's Neck,* 1966, no. 36, repr.

Bibliography:
L. Goodrich, *Homer,* New York, 1944, pp.
141–145, 155, 156, repr. p. 147.

THOMAS EAKINS (1844–1916)

Born in Philadelphia, Eakins enrolled in
the Pennsylvania Academy of the Fine
Arts about 1861. Methodical in approach and a realist by nature, he con-
currently studied anatomy at Jefferson
Medical College. In 1866 he began
three years of study in Paris under the
academician Jean-Léon Gérôme and
the portraitist Bonnat. During a winter

in Spain, he was impressed by the
powerful naturalism of Ribera and
Velásquez as well as by Rembrandt. In
1870 he settled permanently in Philadelphia, resumed his studies at Jefferson College, and commenced to paint
precisely constructed and objectively
realistic portraits and genre subjects.
First instructor of the Life Class at the
Pennsylvania Academy, then its Director in 1882, Eakins resigned in 1886
under pressure for his determined use
of the nude model in mixed classes. He
then formed the Philadelphia Art Students League. Eakins' sporting scenes
are marked by an infinitely structured
clarity. His portraits, never flattering,
approach the insight and painterly
strength of the earlier Rembrandt.

58

Max Schmitt in a Single Scull

Oil on canvas. 32 1/4 x 46 1/4 inches.
Signed and dated on scull in background: *Eakins/1871.*

Painted the year following his return
from Europe, Eakins' painting shows his
boyhood friend, the champion oars-
man, Max Schmitt, coasting on the
Schuylkill River. Eakins himself is in the
scull behind. His masterly draftsman-
ship and almost unreal brilliance of
light create an extraordinarily intense
perception of reality.

Collections:
Max Schmitt, Philadelphia; Mrs. Louis S. M.
Nache, his widow; Mrs. Thomas Eakins,
1930.
The Metropolitan Museum of Art, New
York. Alfred N. Punnett Fund and Gift of
George D. Pratt, 1934.

Exhibitions:
Washington, National Gallery, Chicago, Art
Institute, and Philadelphia Museum, *Eakins,*
1961, no. 6; New York, Metropolitan Mu-
seum, *19th-Century America: Paintings and
Sculpture,* 1970, no. 154, repr.; Boston, MFA,

*Masterpieces of Painting in The Metropoli-
tan Museum,* 1970.

Bibliography:
L. Goodrich, *Eakins,* New York, 1933, p. 163,
no. 44, pl. 5; S. Schendler, *Eakins,* Boston
and Toronto, 1967, pp. 33–37, repr. pl. 34.

THOMAS EAKINS

59

Starting Out After Rail

Oil on canvas. 24 x 20 inches.
Signed and dated on stern of boat:
Eakins 74, and lower left: *Eakins.*

A number of Eakins' paintings concern
bird shooting. Here, his friends, Harry
Young and Sam Helhower sail off across
the Delaware River for a day of rail
shooting on the Philadelphia marsh-
lands. Constructed with characteristic
logic and simplicity, each line and angle
of the boat and its location on the
shimmering blue-brown water is carefully ordered.

Collection:
Purchased from the artist by Miss Janet
Wheeler, Philadelphia, 1915.
Museum of Fine Arts, Boston. Charles Henry
Hayden Fund, 1935.

Exhibitions:
New York, Museum of Modern Art, *Art in
Our Time,* 1939, no. 30, repr.; New York,
Whitney Museum, *Eakins,* 1970; New York,
Metropolitan Museum, *100 Paintings from
the Boston Museum,* 1970, repr.

Bibliography:
C. C. Cunningham, "A Sporting Picture by
Eakins," *Boston MFA Bulletin,* 1936, XXXIV,
no. 201, pp. 11–12, repr. p. 12.

THOMAS EAKINS

60

Lady with a Setter Dog

Oil on canvas. 30 x 23 inches.
Painted in 1885.

The portrait is of Eakins' wife, Susan
Hannah Macdowell (1851–1938), the
daughter of the Philadelphia engraver,

58 EAKINS. Max Schmitt in a Single Scull

59 EAKINS. Starting Out After Rail

60 EAKINS. Lady with a Setter Dog

William H. Macdowell, one of Eakins' students at the Pennsylvania Academy. Painted the year after their marriage, Mrs. Eakins, with the family red setter, Harry, appears in a moment of quiet contemplation in a corner of a room, perhaps his studio. Unlike the crystalline clarity of the outdoor scenes, realism in this extremely personal picture is achieved through the casual yet graceful composition and the unflattering but deeply felt portrayal of the lady.

Collection:
Mrs. Thomas Eakins, Philadelphia.
The Metropolitan Museum of Art, New York. Fletcher Fund, 1923.
Exhibitions:
New York, Metropolitan Museum, *Life in America*, 1939, no. 256; Philadelphia Museum, *Eakins Centennial*, 1944, no. 52; New York, Whitney Museum, *Eakins,* 1970.
Bibliography:
L. Goodrich, *Eakins,* New York, 1933, p. 178, no. 213, pl. 30; S. Schendler, *Eakins,* Boston and Toronto, 1967, pp. 87, 89, 120, 172, fig. 39.

WILLIAM MICHAEL HARNETT
(1848–1892)

Harnett, born in County Cork, Ireland, was brought to Philadelphia as a child, and later worked there and in New York as a silver engraver. He also studied painting at night at the Pennsylvania Academy, the Cooper Union and National Academy in New York, and in 1875 became a painter. He worked at the Pennsylvania Academy from 1876 until 1880, then in Frankfurt and Munich until 1884, returning by way of Paris and London to settle in New York in 1886. While owing an important debt to Raphaelle Peale's early efforts at *trompe l'oeil* painting, Harnett's inherent taste and genius for objective pre-

cision developed that form to its highest point in American art.

61
Old Models

Oil on canvas. 54 x 28 inches.
Signed and dated lower left: *WMHarnett/1892* (initials in monogram).
Old Models, perhaps the last and certainly one of the best of Harnett's paintings, combines monumentality with quiet composure. It contrasts with the aggressive complexity of objects in his great *After the Hunt* (California Palace of the Legion of Honor, San Francisco) and the vivid coloration of the earlier *Card Rack* (no. 61). The painting is familiar throughout the world from its recent reproduction on a six-cent postage stamp.

Collections:
Estate of the artist, 1892; *Harnett Estate Sale,* Thomas Birch's Sons, Philadelphia, Feb. 23–24, 1893, no. 27, repr. frontispiece; *A. Ludwig Collection Sale,* Fifth Avenue Art Galleries, New York, Feb. 1–2, 1898, no. 93; William J. Hughes, Washington, D. C.
Museum of Fine Arts, Boston. Charles Henry Hayden Fund, 1939.
Exhibitions:
San Francisco, California Palace of the Legion of Honor, *Illusionism and Trompe l'Œil,* 1949, repr. p. 33; American Federation of Arts, New York, (circulated in Europe and to Whitney Museum, New York), *American Painting in the Nineteenth Century,* 1953–1954, no. 40.
Bibliography:
A. Frankenstein, *After the Hunt,* Berkeley, Calif., 1953, pp. 89 (note 57), 92, 95, 108, 174, pl. 82.

WILLIAM MICHAEL HARNETT
62
The Artist's Card Rack

Oil on canvas. 30 x 25 inches.
Signed and dated upper left: *WMHarnett/1879* (initials in monogram).

Painted only four years after Harnett had resolved to be an artist, this brilliant and complex picture was thought, until another was discovered in 1969, to be his only letter-rack painting, a frequent theme in Peto's work. Its superb execution and fragmentary references to people and places make the painting provocative both in technique and content.

Collections:
Commissioned by Israel Reifsnyder, Philadelphia; Howard Reifsnyder; sold, American Art Association, New York, 1929, no. 611; Mr. Schinasi; Leonora Schinasi (Mrs. Arthur Hornblow, Jr.), Beverly Hills; Mr. and Mrs. Lawrence A. Fleischman, Detroit, 1958.
The Metropolitan Museum of Art, New York. Morris K. Jesup Fund, 1966.
Exhibitions:
La Jolla Museum of Art and Santa Barbara Museum of Art, *The Reminiscent Object,* 1964–1965, no. 10, repr.; New York, Metropolitan Museum, *19th-Century America: Paintings and Sculpture,* 1970, no. 170, repr.
Bibliography:
A. Frankenstein, *After the Hunt: William Harnett and Other American Still Life Painters, 1870–1900,* Berkeley and Los Angeles, 1969, pp. 50–53, 108, 169, no. 45, repr. pl. 46.

JOHN FREDERICK PETO (1854–1907)

Peto was born in Philadelphia and was painting by 1875. He studied briefly at the Pennsylvania Academy in 1878, but he was primarily self-taught, although an admirer and competitor of William Harnett. In 1889 he settled in Island Heights, N. J. and except for a trip to Lerado, Ohio in 1894 worked there until his death. For many years, Peto's work was confused with that of the more famous Harnett, a confusion compounded by the occasional forging by others of Harnett's signature on Peto's

61 HARNETT. Old Models

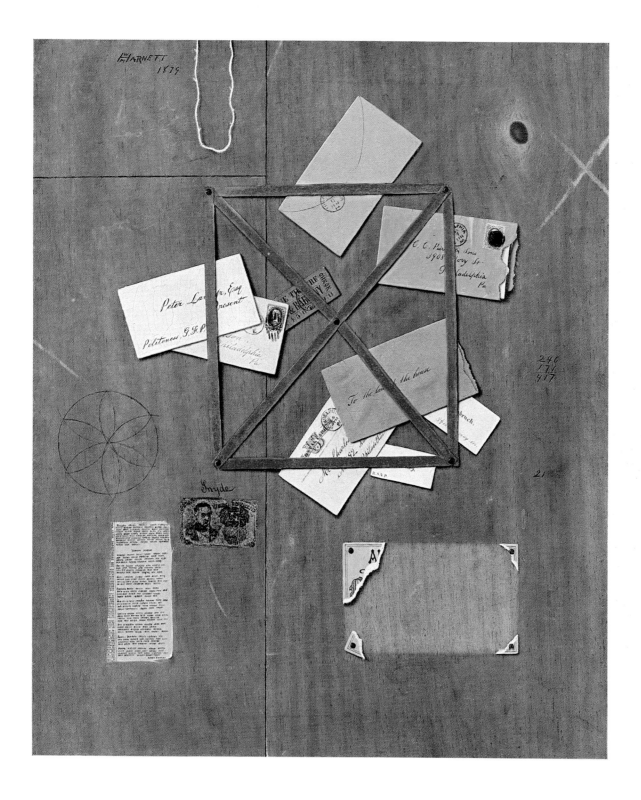

62 HARNETT. The Artist's Card Rack

painting. While superficially alike, significant stylistic differences -- more textural use of pigment and more casual compositions – separate his work from Harnett's.

63
The Poor Man's Store

Oil on canvas and wood.
36 x 25^1/$_2$ inches.
Signed and dated upper left, on the canvas: *J. F. Peto/–85*
Contrasted with Peto's many paintings of card-racks or books, mugs, pipes and the like, *The Poor Man's Store,* even to its title, displays a lighthearted charm and humor unique in his work. Peto has heightened the illusion by painting the window and objects in it on a canvas recessed behind an actual surrounding wooden panel.

Collections:
Private collection, East Orange, N. J.; Mrs. Raymond Dey, Preakness, N. J., about 1940; Miss Mary Allis, Fairfield, Conn., about 1943; Maxim Karolik, Newport, R. I., 1951. Museum of Fine Arts, Boston. M. and M. Karolik Collection, 1962.
Exhibitions:
Northampton, Mass., Smith College Museum, Brooklyn Museum, and San Francisco, California Palace of the Legion of Honor, *Peto,* 1950, no. 4, fig. 7; New York, World's Fair, *Four Centuries of American Masterpieces,* 1964, no. 22, repr.; New York, Metropolitan Museum, *19th-Century America: Paintings and Sculpture,* 1970, no. 181, repr.
Bibliography:
A. Frankenstein, *After the Hunt,* Berkeley and Los Angeles, 1969, pp. 101–102, pl. 84; E. P. Richardson, *Painting in America,* New York, 1956, pp. 322–323, fig. 136.

ELIHU VEDDER (1836–1923)

Born in New York City, Vedder grew up in Schenectady, and had begun to paint by twelve. In 1856, at twenty, he went to Paris to study, then to Florence which, with Rome, was an important center of Romantic art. During the war years in New York, Vedder produced some of his finest romantic-symbolic paintings. In 1866, he returned to Paris, then settled permanently in Rome, despite frequent travels in Europe and to America.

64
Lair of the Sea Serpent

Oil on canvas. 21 x 36 inches.
Signed and dated lower left: *Elihu Vedder/1864.*
Vedder's style, unlike the emotionalism of his contemporaries, Ryder and Blakelock, combined romantic idealizations with an individual quality of mystery. The *Lair of the Sea Serpent* is an extraordinary vision of a menacing sea monster coiled incongruously on a dune under a warm, sunny sky. Its baleful stare and threatening immobility poses an almost impenetrable mystery.

Collection:
Purchased from the artist by Thomas G. Appleton, Boston, 1864–1865. Museum of Fine Arts, Boston. Bequest of Thomas Appleton, 1884.
Exhibitions:
New York, Museum of Modern Art, *Romantic Painting in America,* 1943, p. 29, no. 199, repr. p. 69; New York, Metropolitan Museum, *100 Paintings from the Boston Museum,* 1970.
Bibliography:
E. Vedder, *Digressions of Vedder,* Boston, 1910, p. 463, repr. p. 247; E. P. Richardson, *American Romantic Painting,* New York, 1945, p. 48, no. 208.

RALPH ALBERT BLAKELOCK (1847–1919)

One of the most tragic yet individual figures of American art, Blakelock suffered rejection as an artist, mental illness and increasing poverty through much of his life. He was born in New York, and taught himself painting and drawing. On his journeys through the West between 1869 and 1872, he became fascinated, not by its dramatic vastness as was Bierstadt, but by the Indian and his harmonious assimilation into the life of the forests. His paintings were intensely personal visions of mysterious forest scenes often moodily bathed in moonlight. After a series of mental crises he was confined to an asylum from about 1899 to 1916. During this period his paintings found increasing favor, and in 1916 he was elected to the National Academy.

65
Indian Encampment

Oil on canvas. 37^1/$_2$ x 40^1/$_4$ inches.
Signed, in arrowhead, lower left: *Ralph Albert Blakelock.* Painted probably in the 1870's.
Blakelock's earliest paintings have the bright clarity of early Homer, which following his western journey, was replaced by rough textures and earthy tones. The blonder palette and brightly colored figures here suggests a relatively early date.

Collection:
George A. Hearn, New York, by 1900–1906. The Metropolitan Museum of Art, New York. Gift of George A. Hearn, 1906.
Exhibitions:
New York, Whitney Museum, *Blakelock Centenary,* 1947, p. 45, no. 8, repr. frontispiece; New York, Metropolitan Museum, *19th-Century America: Paintings and Sculpture,* 1970, no. 150, repr.

Facing page
63 PETO. The Poor Man's Store

64 VEDDER. Lair of the Sea Serpent

65 BLAKELOCK. Indian Encampment
66 RYDER. Constance

67 HUNT. Miss Ida Mason

Bibliography:
E. Daingerfield, *Blakelock,* New York, 1914, pp. 28–29, repr. opp. p. 16.

ALBERT PINKHAM RYDER (1847–1917)

Ryder moved from his native New Bedford to New York in 1870. He was essentially self-taught despite brief study at the National Academy of Design and informal instruction from William E. Marshall, a little known portrait painter and engraver. Several short trips to London and Europe also had little effect on his art. While a contemporary of the giants of Realism, Homer and Eakins, Ryder's art was the product of an intensely poetic genius. His often symbolic paintings are dreamlike essences, stripped of detail, that explore the moody inner world of his imagination. His limited production, often in faulty condition from experimental combinations of incompatible materials, received limited acceptance during much of his life. Yet, with Blakelock, he is recognized as one of the major Romantic artists of the nineteenth century.

66
Constance
Oil on canvas. 28$\frac{1}{4}$ x 36 inches.
Completed in 1896.
Literature and music, rather than other paintings, had the greatest influence on Ryder. The works of Shakespeare and especially the Romantic authors, Byron, Tennyson, Poe, and the composer, Richard Wagner, provided the subjects for many of his paintings. Chaucer's *Canterbury Tales* (The Man of Law's Tale) contains a story of ancient injustice and ultimate salvation in which Constance, daughter of a Roman emperor, was abandoned at sea with her infant son on orders of her jealous mother-in-law. Miraculously safeguarded, five years later she reached Rome and future happiness. Ryder has envisioned the frail craft on a broad, quiet sea with moonlight glowing like a protective beam about the boat.

Collections:
Sir William Van Horne, Montreal, before 1905; Lady Van Horne, by 1918; Montreal Art Association.
Museum of Fine Arts, Boston. Abraham Shuman Fund, 1945.
Exhibition:
Washington, D. C., Corcoran Gallery, *Ryder Retrospective,* 1961, no. 56, repr. p. 42.
Bibliography:
L. Goodrich, *Ryder,* New York, 1959, pp. 19, 115, 121, pls. 65–67.

WILLIAM MORRIS HUNT (1824–1879)

Hunt, born in Brattleboro, Vt., attended Harvard but before graduation was taken to Europe for his health. He attempted sculpture in Paris and Rome, tried painting at the Düsseldorf Academy, returned briefly to America in 1846, but left again for Paris to paint under Thomas Couture. Hunt soon was an enthusiast of Jean François Millet and joined him at Barbizon. In 1855, he married a Boston lady, and after some years in Brattleboro and Newport, R. I., settled in Boston. There her position and his enthusiasm for the Barbizon artists helped to establish a number of important collections of Barbizon art and an interest in French painting sustained into the twentieth century. A portrait, landscape and genre painter, Hunt worked in a warm, textural style strongly influenced by Couture and the Barbizon artists.

67
Miss Ida Mason
Oil on canvas. 42 x 30$\frac{1}{4}$ inches.
Signed and dated lower left: *WMH/ 1878* (initials in monogram).
Until the rise of John Singer Sargent in the 1870's, Hunt was the most important painter of Bostonians. His portrait of *Ida Mason,* painted just the year before his accidental death, shows him at the height of his powers as a colorist. He has also sensitively captured her delicate dignity with a simplicity in sharp contrast to Sargent's fashionable sophistication.

Collection:
Museum of Fine Arts, Boston. Charles Henry Hayden Fund, 1932.
Exhibition:
American Federation of Arts, New York (circulated in Europe and to Whitney Museum, New York), *American Painting in the Nineteenth Century,* 1953–1954, no. 42.
Bibliography:
M. A. S. Shannon, *Hunt,* Boston, 1923, repr. opp. p. 100.

JOHN SINGER SARGENT (1856–1925)

Born in Florence of well-to-do American parents, Sargent traveled widely through Europe with them and, showing talent, enrolled at the Academy of Fine Arts in Florence in 1870 at only fourteen. In Dresden from 1871 to 1872, he visited Venice in 1874 where Whistler offered strong encouragement. That year the family settled in Paris where he studied under the fashionable portraitist Carolus-Duran. Sargent then made the first of many trips to America, establishing an enduring rapport with the society of Boston and New York. Later, in Italy, Spain and Holland, he was deeply influenced by the paintings of Hals and Velasquez. By the early 1880's he became the most fashionable portrait painter of Boston, New York and London, yet also produced throughout

68 SARGENT. Rehearsal of the Pasdeloup Orchestra at the Cirque d'Hiver

his career exceptional genre and landscape paintings in both oil and brilliant watercolors.

68
Rehearsal of the Pasdeloup Orchestra at the Cirque d'Hiver
Oil on canvas. $21^3/_4 \times 18^1/_4$ inches.
Inscribed lower right: *Rehearsal at the Cirque/d'Hiver/John S. Sargent.*
Painted in 1876.

Although painted when only twenty, this monochrome masterpiece already reveals Sargent's precocious genius. The unusual vantage point, special touches such as the bass player at the left and the crouching tympanist silhouetted against his drum, as well as the subject itself, all suggest a debt to Degas. Conductor Jules Etienne Pasdeloup's orchestra held rehearsals in the Cirque d'Hiver for their popular concerts at the Théâtre des Champs-Elysées.

Collections:
Acquired from the artist by Henry Bacon, London; Mrs. Henry Bacon.
Museum of Fine Arts, Boston. Charles Henry Hayden Fund, 1922.
Exhibitions:
Boston, MFA, *Sargent Memorial,* 1925, no. 3; Washington, D. C., Corcoran Gallery, and circulated in the U.S., *Private World of John Singer Sargent,* 1964–1965, no. 1, repr.
Bibliography:
E. Charteris, *Sargent,* New York, 1927, pp. 43, 223, 280, repr. opp. p. 32.

JOHN SINGER SARGENT
69
Madame X – Madame Pierre Gautreau
Oil on canvas. $82^1/_8 \times 43^1/_4$ inches.
Signed and dated lower right: *John S. Sargent 1884.*
Sargent's famous portrait of the notorious Parisian beauty, Madame Pierre Gautreau, created a great critical and popular uproar when first exhibited in the Paris Salon of 1884, both for her scandalous costume and his rendering of her customary heavy lavendar make-up. Formerly Judith Avegno of New Orleans, she married a Parisian banker, and during the 1880's tantalized and outraged society. After ultimately consenting to sit for Sargent, her temperament and his struggle for an appropriate artistic concept prolonged completion. Yet after many attempts, Sargent has inventively and daringly captured her beauty, vanity and audacity.

Collection:
Purchased from the artist, 1916.
The Metropolitan Museum of Art, New York. Arthur H. Hearn Fund, 1916.
Exhibitions:
Chicago, Art Institute, and New York, Metropolitan Museum, *Sargent, Whistler and Cassatt,* 1954, no. 49; New York, Metropolitan Museum, *19th-Century America: Paintings and Sculpture,* 1970, no. 178, repr.; Boston, MFA, *Masterpieces of Painting in The Metropolitan Museum,* 1970.
Bibliography:
E. Charteris, *Sargent,* New York, 1927, pp. 59–65.

JOHN SINGER SARGENT
70
Mrs. Fiske Warren and Her Daughter
Oil on canvas. $60 \times 40^1/_4$ inches.
Signed and dated lower left: *John S. Sargent. 1903.*
The portrait of Gretchen Osgood Warren (1871–1961) and her daughter, Rachel, one of Sargent's most gracious and sensitive later paintings, displays neither the crisp, bold directness of his magnificent early group portrait of the *Daughters of Edward Darley Boit,* 1882 (Museum of Fine Arts, Boston), nor the haughty sophistication of some of his London portraits. The broken color of their shimmering pink dresses conveys a sensitive softness matching the sitters' own tender relationship. The portrait was painted in the Gothic Room of Fenway Court, the fabulous Venetian-style villa built in Boston by Sargent's patron, Mrs. Jack Gardner.

Collections:
Fiske Warren, Brookline, Mass.; Mrs. Fiske Warren, Boston, 1938; Mrs. Rachel Warren Barton and Hamilton Warren, 1961.
Museum of Fine Arts, Boston. Gift of Rachel Warren Barton and the Emily L. Ainsley Fund, 1964.
Exhibitions:
Boston, MFA, *Sargent Memorial,* 1925, no. 80; Cleveland Museum, *American Painting from 1860 Until Today,* 1937, p. 38, repr. frontispiece.
Bibliography:
W. H. Downes, *Sargent,* Boston, 1925, p. 210, repr. opp. p. 248.

JAMES ABBOTT McNEILL WHISTLER (1834–1903)
Whistler, born in Lowell, Mass., was a reluctant student, failed to graduate from West Point and became a technical draftsman for two years. In Charles Gleyre's Paris studio in 1856, Whistler became deeply involved in the city's tumultuous art life. His ardent admiration for Courbet appears in the powerfully structured and earthy tones of his earlier work. In 1863 he moved to London, where he remained except for occasional trips and another period in Paris from 1892 to 1898. During the later sixties and seventies, partly prompted by early Impressionism and newly discovered Japanese art, he developed an increasing preoccupation with purely aesthetic concerns. Subject matter became a vehicle for internal considerations of form, composition, and color. His title designations, Harmonies,

69 SARGENT. Madame X – Madame Pierre Gautreau

70 SARGENT. Mrs. Fiske Warren and Her Daughter

71 WHISTLER. The Lagoon, Venice: Nocturne in Blue and Silver

Compositions, and Nocturnes, underline that aesthetic emphasis.

71

The Lagoon, Venice:
Nocturne in Blue and Silver

Oil on canvas. 20 x 25^3/$_4$ inches.
Signed lower left with butterfly symbol.
Painted in 1879–1880.
Created during Whistler's Venetian visit of 1879–1880, *The Lagoon* records the soft atmospheric nuances of that splendid harbor by night. More importantly, the work is primarily a pictorial composition in harmonies of muted blues, in essence a proto-abstract color concept.

Collections:
Sold, Hôtel Drouot, Paris, Nov. 25, 1903, no. 1; Richard A. Canfield, Providence, R. I., 1904; Mrs. William H. Bliss, New York, 1914; Mrs. Robert Woods Bliss, her daughter, Washington, D. C.
Museum of Fine Arts, Boston. Emily L. Ainsley Fund, 1942.
Exhibitions:
London, Arts Council Gallery and New York, M. Knoedler and Co., *Whistler*, 1960, no. 43; Berlin, Nationalgalerie, *Whistler*, 1969, p. 78, no. 33, repr. p. 54.
Bibliography:
E. R. and J. Pennell, *Whistler*, Philadelphia, 1908, I, pp. 266–267.

WILLIAM MERRITT CHASE
(1849–1916)

Chase was born in Williamsburg (now Nineveh), Ind., received some training in Indianapolis, then entered the National Academy of Design in New York in 1869. From 1872 to 1877 he worked at the Royal Academy in Munich, then in Venice with Duveneck and Twachtman. He settled in New York in 1878, taught at the Art Students League, the Brooklyn Art School and the Art Institute of Chicago among others. He made numerous trips to Europe, especially to Spain, Paris and London, and was greatly impressed by the painting of Velasquez. Chase joined the Ten American Painters group in 1902, but while his art reveals an awareness of Impressionism, his interests were diverse and reflect as much the impact of Whistler and Sargent.

72

James Abbott McNeill Whistler

Oil on canvas. 74^3/$_8$ x 36^1/$_4$ inches.
Signed, dated and inscribed upper left: *To my friend Whistler/Wm M. Chase/ London 1885.*
Chase met Whistler in London in 1885 and a spontaneous if brief friendship developed. They quickly resolved to paint each other's portrait, and while Whistler's is lost, Chase's is a brilliantly incisive portrayal. Chase wrote of two distinct aspects of Whistler's personality: "One was Whistler in public – the fop, the cynic, the brilliant, flippant, vain and careless idler; the other was Whistler of the studio – the earnest, tireless sombre worker, a very slave to his art, a bitter foe of all pretense and sham …"

Collection:
William H. Walker, New York.
The Metropolitan Museum of Art, New York. Bequest of William H. Walker, 1918.
Exhibitions:
Santa Barbara, Art Gallery, University of California, and circulated in the U. S., *Chase*, 1964, no. 10, repr.
Bibliography:
E. R. and J. Pennell, *Whistler*. Philadelphia, 1908, II, pp. 29–30; K. M. Roof, *The Life and Art of William Merritt Chase*, New York, 1917, pp. 111–149, 207 (Notes).

MARY CASSATT (1844–1926)

Mary Stevenson Cassatt, one of America's most famous artists, was born to a well-to-do-family in Allegheny City, Pa., near Pittsburgh and grew up in Philadelphia. Determined to be a painter, she attended the Pennsylvania Academy but, frustrated by the teaching regimen, left for France in 1866, also toured Italy, Spain and The Lowlands, then settled in Paris. Essentially self-taught, she joined the young Impressionist group on the invitation of Degas, who became a lifelong friend and adviser. Although close to Manet and Berthe Morisot as well, she developed a personal style which, while guided by Degas, was also strongly influenced by Japanese prints. In addition to her paintings, her rich pastels and firmly drawn prints are exceptional. Her close association with important collectors in Boston, New York and Philadelphia, especially Mr. and Mrs. H. O. Havemeyer, was instrumental in early acceptance of Impressionist art in America. After 1910, increasing blindness ended her career and she died at her Château de Beaufresne (Oise).

73
The Cup of Tea
Oil on canvas. 25$\frac{1}{2}$ x 36$\frac{1}{2}$ inches. Signed lower left: *Mary Cassatt*. Painted about 1880.
On the left, the artist's sister, Lydia, rather pensively takes tea with a young visitor at the summer villa in Marly-le-Roi. The gleaming Philadelphia silver service, a gift of the artist's grandmother, is a rich foil to the softly textured reds and grays of the interior. Although fully in the Impressionist manner, the firm, clear modeling of the figures is an essential element of her style.

73 CASSATT. The Cup of Tea

74 HASSAM. Boston Common at Twilight

Collections:
Henri Rouart, Paris; sold Galerie Manzi-Joyant, Paris, Dec. 9–11, 1912, no. 91; Dikran G. Kelekian, Paris.
Museum of Fine Arts, Boston. Maria Hopkins Fund, 1942.

Exhibitions:
Paris, *Fifth Impressionist Exhibition,* 1880; Baltimore Museum, *Manet, Degas, Cassatt, Morisot,* 1962, no. 102, repr. p. 40; New York, Metropolitan Museum, *100 Paintings from the Boston Museum,* 1970.

Bibliography:
B. N. Parker, "A Philadelphian in Paris," *Boston MFA Bulletin,* 1942, no. 240, p. 63, repr.; F. A. Sweet, *Miss Mary Cassatt: Impressionist from Philadelphia,* Norman, Okla., 1966, p. 51, color pl. III.

FREDERICK CHILDE HASSAM
(1859–1935)

Frederick Childe Hassam, raised in the Boston area, was first an illustrator for a Boston wood-engraver, but began portrait painting under the minor but popular emigrant Bavarian artist, Ignaz Gaugengigl. Although in Europe in 1883, his years in Paris from 1886 to 1889 were of far greater impact. At first in the conservative milieu of the Académie Julian, Hassam soon abandoned the muted realism of his American style for the vibrant spontaneity of Impressionism. He became quite successful on returning to New York, and with Twachtman, Theodore Robinson, and others, later formed the Impressionist-oriented "Ten American Painters" group. He lived in New York but made regular summer trips to his favorite New England haunts, about Greenwich, Conn., Gloucester, Mass., and the Isle of Shoals, N. H.

74
Boston Common at Twilight
Oil on canvas. 42 x 60 inches.

Signed and dated lower right: *Childe Hassam/1885–6.*
This view of the Common on a winter evening is in the Realist tradition of Homer and Eastman Johnson, yet it glows with a luminous light and atmosphere gained from the paintings of George Inness. One of the finest of Hassam's earlier American paintings, the work already reveals a sophisticated control of color.

Collections:
Mr. Appleton, Boston, by about 1895; Miss Maud E. Appleton, Boston, by 1927.
Museum of Fine Arts, Boston. Gift of Miss Maud E. Appleton, 1931.

Exhibition:
Washington, D. C., Corcoran Gallery, and circulated in the U. S., *Hassam,* 1965, no. 3, repr. p. 10.

FREDERICK CHILDE HASSAM
75
Grand Prix Day
Oil on canvas. 24 x 34 inches.
Signed and dated lower left: *Childe Hassam Paris – 1887.*
On a busy thoroughfare near the Place de l'Etoile, with a glimpse of the Arc de Triomphe at the left, fashionable ladies and gentlemen promenade in their coaches and carriages on race day. Painted little more than a year after the relatively sombre *Boston Common* (no. 74), this painting sparkles with the color and vitality of Impressionism. City views dominated Hassam's earlier work, but on returning from Paris, he painted almost exclusively brightly and broadly executed landscapes, often enlivened with figures bathed in sunlight.

Collections:
Celian M. Spitzer, Toledo, Ohio, about 1900; Sidney Spitzer, a collateral descendant, 1919.
Museum of Fine Arts, Boston. Ernest Wadsworth Longfellow Fund, 1964.

Exhibitions:
Washington, D. C., Corcoran Gallery, and circulated in the U. S., *Hassam,* 1965, no. 5, repr. p. 12; New York, Metropolitan Museum, *19th-Century America: Paintings and Sculpture,* 1970, no. 183, repr.

JOHN HENRY TWACHTMAN
(1853–1902)

Twachtman, born in Cincinnati, decorated windowshades for his father, while also taking drawing lessons at the Ohio Mechanics Institute. He later worked under Frank Duveneck and in 1875 accompanied him for two years' study at the Munich Academy. They then joined William Merritt Chase in Venice for a year. Twachtman returned to New York but later worked with Duveneck in Florence, toured Holland, and from 1883 to 1885 studied at the Académie Julian in Paris. In 1889 he settled in Greenwich, Conn., which became an informal center for the Impressionist-oriented group, the Ten American Painters, which included Hassam, Chase, and J. Alden Weir. Although one of its most important members, Twachtman's sensitive atmospheric paintings have begun to receive their proper attention only in recent years.

76
Arques-La-Bataille
Oil on canvas. 60 x 78⁷/₈ inches.
Signed and dated lower left:
J. H. TWACHTMAN./1885/PARIS.
In this major painting from Twachtman's period in Paris, he has abandoned the more emphatic darkly colored style derived from his Munich experience in favor of softly tinted tonal harmonies, probably as a consequence of exposure to the painting of Whistler and to Japanese prints. A similar poetic sensitivity with an increasingly broad

75 HASSAM. Grand Prix Day

76 TWACHTMAN. Arques-La-Bataille

handling of pigment characterizes his later production.

Collections:
Mrs. John H. Twachtman, Greenwich, Conn.; Dr. Eric Twachtman, Essex, Conn.
The Metropolitan Museum of Art, New York. Morris K. Jesup Fund, 1968.

Exhibitions:
Cincinnati Art Museum, *Twachtman*, 1966, pp. 8, 13, no. 29, repr.; New York, Metropolitan Museum, *19th-Century America: Paintings and Sculpture,* 1970, no. 182, repr.

Bibliography:
E. Clark, *Twachtman,* New York, 1924, pp. 25, 38.

ROBERT HENRI (1865–1929)

Henri, born in Cincinnati, studied under Thomas Anshutz, Eakins' successor at the Pennsylvania Academy in Philadelphia. After two years there, Henri enrolled at the Académie Julian in Paris, in 1888 and 1889, then worked independently until returning to Philadelphia in 1891 to teach. An articulate theoretician and teacher, Henri attracted to himself several Philadelphia artists, including John Sloan, George Luks, and William Glackens, often commercial illustrators and former pupils of Anshutz, who shared his desire to revitalize the Realist tradition by focusing on the realities of modern urban life. He settled in New York in 1899, followed by Sloan, Luks, and Glackens. By 1908 the group, enlarged by such disparate artists as Maurice Prendergast, Everett Shinn, and Ernest Lawson, became identified as The Eight or Ashcan School, for their broadly handled views of the seamy side of city life. While not the strongest painter of the group, Henri's aesthetic inspiration was pivotal to their development. In later years he returned frequently to Europe and painted numbers of skillful but occasionally saccharine portraits.

77 HENRI. The Masquerade Dress: Portrait of Mrs. Robert Henri

77
The Masquerade Dress:
Portrait of Mrs. Robert Henri
Oil on canvas. 76½ x 36¼ inches.
Signed lower right: *Robert Henri.*
Painted in 1911.
There is much of Manet in this formal
but graceful portrait of Henri's wife:
the solid planes of color, strong light
separating the figure from a dark, undefined background and a direct sense
of life and movement. Mrs. Henri, a
graphic artist and watercolor painter
herself, exhibited under her maiden
name, Marjorie Organ.

Collection:
Miss Violet Organ, New York.
The Metropolitan Museum of Art, New
York. Arthur H. Hearn Fund, 1958.
Exhibition:
Brooklyn Museum, *Face of America,* 1957–
1958, fig. 36.
Bibliography:
H. Geldzahler, *American Painting in the
20th Century,* New York, 1965, p. 21, repr.
p. 20.

JOHN SLOAN (1871–1951)
Sloan, born in Lock Haven, Pa.,
studied like Shinn and Henri, at the
Pennsylvania Academy under Thomas
Anshutz. In 1894, he began work as a
newspaper illustrator in Philadelphia,
as did several future members of The
Eight. In 1904 he moved to New York to
become a freelance illustrator, and exhibited with The Eight in 1908. Despite
the intellectual leadership of Henri, it
was Sloan and Luks who remained most
consistent to the concept of social realism. Sloan was later active as a teacher
at the Art Students League.

78
Pigeons
Oil on canvas. 26 x 32 inches.

78 SLOAN. Pigeons

Signed and dated lower right: *John Sloan/1910.*

The broad, blunt brushwork of Sloan's painting, similar to that of Luks, Henri, Glackens and others of the Ashcan group, injected a new immediacy to the American Realist tradition. Paintings of life in the tenements and streets of New York were a radical development in American art, even if less extreme than the contemporary European works in the famous Armory Show of 1913. Arthur B. Davies, a member of The Eight, was the principal organizer of that exhibition.

Collection:
Museum of Fine Arts, Boston. Charles Henry Hayden Fund, 1935.
Exhibitions:
New York, 24–31 West 35th Street, *Independent Artists*, 1910, no. 69; New York, Whitney Museum, and circulated in the U. S., *Sloan*, 1952, no. 24.
Bibliography:
J. Sloan, *Gist of Art*, New York, 1939, repr. p. 222.

MAURICE PRENDERGAST (1859–1924)

Maurice Brazil Prendergast, born in St. John's, Newfoundland and brought to Boston as a child, centered his life about that city. He began to sketch and paint about 1887 and two years later made the first of many trips to Europe. In 1891 he studied at the Académie Julian with Laurens, but it was the Impressionists, especially Boudin, and the Post-Impressionist group called the Nabis, led by Bonnard and Vuillard, which oriented his work. In 1894, Prendergast settled in Winchester, near Boston, later worked in Boston and finally moved to New York in 1914. Although a member of The Eight, his gaily colorful paintings differ markedly from their sort of social realism. For many years interest in Prendergast was limited, yet in recent times, the quality of his work and his significance for the development of modern art has become appreciated.

79
Eight Bathers
Oil on canvas. 28 1/4 x 24 inches.
Signed bottom center: *Prendergast.*
Painted about 1916–1918.
Prendergast, like Whistler, was concerned with painting as art, not subject matter. His vibrant painting of nude bathers is an essay in pure color and overall decoration. These works in which figures are reduced to shapes distributed about a spaceless picture surface indirectly anticipate Abstract Impressionism.

Collection:
Mrs. Charles Prendergast, the artist's sister-in-law, Westport, Conn.
Museum of Fine Arts, Boston. Abraham Shuman Fund, 1961.
Exhibition:
Boston, MFA, and circulated in the U. S., *Maurice Prendergast*, 1960–1961, no. 38, repr. p. 14.

MARSDEN HARTLEY (1877–1943)

Hartley was one of the first American painters, most of them in the group surrounding the pivotal photographer-artist-dealer Alfred Stieglitz, to absorb himself in the new modernism. Born in Lewiston, Maine, raised there and in Cleveland, he entered the National Academy in New York in 1898, studying under William Merritt Chase, among others. In Paris and Berlin between 1912 and 1915, he was exposed first to the intellectual Cubist style, but was more instinctively receptive to the primitivistic and emotional work of the German Expressionists. On returning to America, he worked in a highly per-

Facing page
79 PRENDERGAST. Eight Bathers

80 HARTLEY. Carnival of Autumn

sonal style of symbolic abstraction, but in later years, which included frequent trips to Europe and the American Southwest, he returned to a naturalistic but powerfully economical style using bold outlines and luminous color. He died in Ellsworth, Maine.

80
Carnival of Autumn

Oil on canvas. 30$\frac{1}{4}$ x 30$\frac{1}{8}$ inches.
Painted in 1908.

The intensification of color and decorative ordering of stylized shapes of Hartley's early landscape reflect his awareness of European Post-Impressionist painting styles, particularly that of the Symbolists. The mountains of Maine persisted as a major theme in Hartley's art, but in later years were conceived in less colorful and more moodily dramatic terms.

Collection:
Hudson D. Walker.
Museum of Fine Arts, Boston. Charles Henry Hayden Fund, 1968.
Exhibition:
Boston, MFA, *Centennial Acquisitions: Art Treasures for Tomorrow,* 1970, no. 97, repr. color p. 136.
Bibliography:
E. McCausland, *Hartley,* Minneapolis, 1952, pp. 13–14, repr. p. 10.

GEORGE BELLOWS (1882–1925)

George Wesley Bellows, born in Columbus, Ohio, joined the group around Robert Henri at the New York School of Art in 1904. His landscapes and city views in the decade following were very much in the matter of Henri's realism, direct and active. His career advanced rapidly and he was soon teaching at the Art Students League and later at the School of the Art Institute of Chicago. An organizer of the Armory Show of 1913 in New York, the work of the Cubists shown there and study of Dynamic Symmetry with Jay Hambridge stimulated a more simplified formalism in his work. Bellows never visited Europe, and while his winter base remained in New York, he summered in the art colonies of Carmel, Calif., Woodstock, N.Y. and Newport, R.I.

81
Emma and Her Children

Oil on canvas. 59 x 65 inches.
Painted in 1923.

This fine, mature work of the artist's wife with their daughters, Anne and Jean, conveys the strength with which Bellows sustained the Realist tradition. The cool tonalities, simplified structure and balanced organization of silently monumental shapes also prefigure the developments of Edward Hopper.

Collections:
Mrs. George Bellows, New York; Boston Art Club.
Museum of Fine Arts, Boston. Gift of Subscribers and the John Lowell Gardner Fund, 1925.
Exhibitions:
Chicago, Art Institute, *Bellows,* 1946, no. 52, repr. p. 54; New York, Gallery of Modern Art, *Bellows,* 1966, no. 68, repr. p. 40; New York, Metropolitan Museum, *100 Paintings from the Boston Museum,* 1970, repr.
Bibliography:
E. S. Bellows, *Paintings of Bellows,* New York, 1929, no. 129, repr.

EDWARD HOPPER (1882–1967)

Hopper, born in Nyack, N.Y., first studied commercial art, but from 1900 to 1906 worked at the New York School of Art under Robert Henri and Kenneth Hayes Miller. Three European trips in the next four years, primarily to Paris,

81 BELLOWS. Emma and Her Children

82 HOPPER. Room in Brooklyn

introduced him to current European movements, the Impressionists in particular, but the broad sure hand of Manet interested him most. In America again, specific Impressionist characteristics fell away, and Hopper developed a basic and economic version of objective realism, shaped in bold, simple, solid forms in sharp clear light. Whether landscape, empty streets, or people at work, they share a common mood of lonely isolation. Also an etcher and outstanding watercolorist, Hopper continued to live in New York with summers on the New England coast.

82
Room in Brooklyn

Oil on canvas. 29 x 34 inches.
Signed lower right: *Edward Hopper.*
Painted in 1932.
This painting is one of Hopper's most compelling statements on the human condition in an urban society. The silent, lonely isolation of this anonymous figure surveying a barren stretch of buildings, is made more powerful by the angular severity of the interior, relieved only by the faint cheer of the flowers. Yet, while deeply felt, his understatement reveals neither sentimentality nor social outrage.

Collection:
Museum of Fine Arts, Boston. Charles Henry Hayden Fund, 1935.
Exhibitions:
New York, Whitney Museum, Chicago, Art Institute, Detroit Institute of Arts and St. Louis, City Art Museum, *Hopper,* 1964–1965, no. 28, repr.; Washington, D.C., National Collection of Fine Arts, for the São Paolo Bienal, Brazil, and Waltham, Mass., Brandeis University, *Hopper,* 1967–1968.

EDWARD HOPPER
83
Tables for Ladies

Oil on canvas. $48^{1}/_{4}$ x $60^{1}/_{4}$ inches.
Signed lower right: *Edward Hopper.*
Painted in 1930.
Hopper portrays night figures such as these with his profound sense of lonely detachment. The people seem not individuals but types, solidly and realistically carrying out the humdrum of life.

Collection:
The Metropolitan Museum of Art. George A. Hearn Fund, 1931.
Exhibition:
Washington, D. C., National Collection of Fine Arts, for the São Paolo Bienal, Brazil, and Waltham, Mass., Brandeis University, *Hopper,* 1967–1968.
Bibliography:
H. Geldzahler, "Edward Hopper," *Metropolitan Museum Bulletin,* November, 1962, p. 117, fig. 5.

JOSEPH STELLA (1879–1946)

Stella, who emigrated from Italy in 1896, began to study art two years later, but first worked as a magazine illustrator. On his frequent trips to Europe he became involved with successive new movements: first Cubism, then Orphism, the formal analysis of color and light in painting. Italian Futurism, a volatile variant of Cubism, dominated his work from 1913 to 1923, when he produced his finest paintings. The Futurists' fascination with the dynamism and speed of mechanistic modern life touched a corresponding chord in Stella's perception of industrial America. His paintings of the period are composed of swirling lines and fractured planes of vivid color. His later work is calmer, more precise and increasingly symbolic and mystical.

84
Coney Island

Oil on canvas. Diameter $41^{3}/_{4}$ inches.
Signed lower right: *Jos. Stella.* Painted about 1915.
The painting curiously combines the frenetic color and light of Futurism with a representation of the Madonna seated at the foot of the cross. The flash and frenzy of Coney Island, and also the mechanical triumph of the Brooklyn Bridge with the visual interlace of its supports, were the two dominant themes of Stella's Futurist work.

Collection:
Chaim Gross, New York.
The Metropolitan Museum of Art, New York. George A. Hearn Fund, 1963.
Exhibitions:
New York, Whitney Museum, *Joseph Stella,* 1963, repr.; Boston, MFA, *Masterpieces of Painting in The Metropolitan Museum,* 1970, repr.
Bibliography:
H. Geldzahler, *American Painting in the 20th Century,* New York, 1965, pp. 69–70, repr. p. 70.

CHARLES SHEELER (1883–1965)

Born in Philadelphia, Sheeler first studied at the School of Industrial Art, then with William Merritt Chase at the Pennsylvania Academy. On several early trips to Europe he was struck by the order of Italian Renaissance painting, especially the geometric logic of Piero della Francesca, and was also exposed to Cubism. In Philadelphia from 1910 to 1919, he began to experiment with photography, and became a highly skilled professional. Sheeler was a leader of the Precisionist group which included Charles Demuth and Preston Dickenson. A variant of the Realist tradition, Precisionism manifested a deep

83 HOPPER. Tables for Ladies

84 STELLA. Coney Island

85 SHEELER. View of New York

86 FEININGER. Regler Church, Erfurt

admiration for the clean lines and basic structures of industrial forms. His later and more colorful paintings became increasingly abstract and dynamic.

85
View of New York

Oil on canvas. 47³/₄ x 36¹/₄ inches.
Signed and dated lower left: *Sheeler – 1931*.

Sheeler has composed the simple elements of his sparse studio, the chair, the dark mass of the camera, within a geometric framework. While the artist himself described the painting as "uncompromising" and the "most severe picture I ever painted," he remains preoccupied with the purity and clarity of mechanical shapes.

Collection:
Museum of Fine Arts, Boston. Charles Henry Hayden Fund, 1935.

Exhibitions:
Minneapolis, Walker Art Center, and circulated in the U.S., *The Precisionist View of American Art*, 1960–1961, p. 58; Washington, D.C., National Collection of Fine Arts, Philadelphia Museum, and New York, Whitney Museum, *Sheeler*, 1968–1969, p. 47, no. 62, repr. p. 49.

Bibliography:
C. Rourke, *Sheeler*, New York, 1938, p. 156, repr. p. 103.

LYONEL FEININGER (1871–1956)

Lyonel Charles Feininger was born in New York, but as a child moved to Germany with his family. He first studied music in 1887, but abandoned it for painting, studying first in Hamburg, then at the Berlin Academy until 1891, and in Paris under Colarossi until 1893. He worked as a newspaper cartoonist and illustrator until 1907, but continued to develop his painting. First under the influence of Delaunay's Cubist-based

Orphism, Feininger later joined the Blaue Reiter Expressionist group with Klee and Kandinsky in 1913. He then joined the highly influential Bauhaus group, teaching painting and graphics at Weimar and Dessau from 1919 until 1932. He returned to New York in 1937 and remained in America until his death.

86
Regler Church, Erfurt

Oil on canvas. 50 x 40¹/₄ inches.
Signed upper left: *Feininger*. Painted in 1930.

Feininger has refracted the shapes of the medieval church in Erfurt into sensitively orchestrated planes of light and color producing a vision of luminosity and grandeur. While the stylistic foundation is Cubist, the painting is a subtle blend of romantic warmth with objective order.

Collections:
Magistrate of Dessau, Germany; Anhaltisches Landesmuseum, Dessau until 1939; G. David Thompson, Pittsburgh, 1953. Museum of Fine Arts, Boston. Charles Henry Hayden Fund, 1957.

Exhibitions:
Cleveland Museum, and circulated in the U.S., *Feininger Memorial*, 1959–1961, no. 42; New York, Metropolitan Museum, *100 Paintings from the Boston Museum*, 1970, repr.

Bibliography:
H. Hess, *Feininger*, New York, 1961, p. 146, no. 324.

WALT KUHN (1877–1949)

Walter Francis Kuhn was born in Brooklyn, N.Y. to German immigrant parents. He studied painting in Paris and Munich from 1901 to 1903 but worked as a cartoonist and illustrator. In 1908 he taught at the New York School of Art with

Robert Henri and established his long friendship with Arthur B. Davies, whom he assisted in organizing the Armory Show. Despite his admiration for modern European painting and temporary absorption of Impressionist and Post-Impressionist styles, Kuhn's art remained essentially American in its direct, Realist approach. Kuhn lived permanently in New York after 1919 but traveled on several occasions to Europe.

87
Clown with Black Wig

Oil on canvas. 40 x 30 inches.
Signed and dated lower left: *Walt Kuhn/1930*.

Similar to Henri, Bellows and Hopper, Kuhn also painted unheroic elements of modern life, but chose acrobats, dancers and still life, painted in basic, massive terms. Not simply objective, his paintings, especially of circus people, are boldly drawn and brightly colored, and contain an inner power akin to the German Expressionists, Beckmann and Nolde.

Collection:
Maynard Walker, New York.
The Metropolitan Museum of Art, New York. George A. Hearn Fund, 1956.

Exhibition:
New York, Metropolitan Museum, *Three Centuries of American Painting*, 1965.

Bibliography:
H. Geldzahler, *American Painting in the 20th Century*, New York, 1965, pp. 81–82, repr. p. 81.

MILTON AVERY (1893–1965)

Avery moved from his birthplace, Altmar, N.Y., to Hartford, Conn. at twelve, and later received his only art training there. After 1925 he lived in New York except for summer trips to rural New York and New England. The work of

87   KUHN. Clown with Black Wig

88 AVERY. Marsden Hartley

Matisse and Albert Marquet, seen in New York in the thirties, were primary influences on his painting: the decorative arrangement of broad, simplified color planes. A great master of color, his paintings, which approach abstraction, are subtle harmonies of delicately atmospheric areas of color. His lyrical compositions had a significant impact on several of the young New York abstractionists, Mark Rothko and Adolph Gottlieb in particular.

88
Marsden Hartley
Oil on canvas. 36 x 28 inches.
Signed and dated lower right: *Milton Avery 1943*.
This compelling and deeply felt portrait of Avery's friend (see no. 80), painted in the year of Hartley's death, stands apart from the mainstream of his style and mood. The painting is almost Expressionist in its portrayal of the intense, brooding face; one almost tangibly feels the physical decay and mental conflict. Avery's skilled selection of acidic color combinations of ghostly yellow-greens and lavender enforces the intensity of mood.

Collection:
Estate of the artist, New York.
Museum of Fine Arts, Boston. Charles Henry Hayden Fund, 1965.
Exhibition:
Lincoln, Neb., Sheldon Memorial Art Gallery, and Little Rock, Arkansas Art Center, *Avery*, 1966, no. 10.
Bibliography:
H. Kramer, *Milton Avery: Paintings 1930–1960*, New York, 1962, p. 73, repr.

EDWIN DICKINSON (born 1891)
Dickinson, born in central New York state, studied under William Merritt Chase in New York, but was more influenced by the portraitist, Charles Hawthorne, his teacher during summers at Provincetown. While Dickinson has made several visits to Europe and the Near East, his painting style, while polished and sophisticated, has remained essentially American. His is a personal and romantic vision of realism, affected somewhat by the mystic inventions of Surrealism. Although his persistent naturalism seems anachronistic in an age of abstraction, renewed vitality in figurative art in the past decade has brought about significant reappraisal.

89
Ruin at Daphne
Oil on canvas. 48 x 60 1/4 inches.
Signed and dated left edge: *E W Dickinson 1943–1953*.
According to the artist, the painting was inspired by the Roman ruins seen at Arles in 1937. From those ancient monuments, he has developed a mysterious environment in which fragments of architecture are composed in decorative yet impossible relationships. By moving from clarity to obscurity, he manipulates the perception of space and the very reality of the scene.

Collection:
The Metropolitan Museum of Art, New York. Edward Joseph Gallagher III Memorial Collection, 1953.
Exhibition:
New York, Whitney Museum, *Edwin Dickinson*, 1966, pp. 16–18, 19, 51, no. 98, repr. p. 42 (unfinished state), p. 43.
Bibliography:
Elaine de Kooning, "Edwin Dickinson Paints a Picture," *Art News,* Sept., 1949, pp. 26 f., repr.; "America, 1953: for the Metropolitan," *Art News*, March, 1955, p. 47, repr.

ANDREW WYETH (born 1917)
Unquestionably the most widely acclaimed living American artist, Wyeth is also part of a dynasty. He was born in Chadds Ford, Pa., where he still lives part of the year, the son of N. C. Wyeth, a famed illustrator of an earlier day. Wyeth's own son, Jamie, has also been applauded as an artist of distinction. Intensive training in drawing under his father guided Andrew Wyeth's own exceptional talents as a draftsman to a level of realism unparalleled in our time. He learned tempera painting from his brother-in-law, Peter Hurd. The subjects of his paintings are confined almost exclusively to the vicinity of Chadds Ford or his summer home in Cushing, Maine.

90
A Crow Flew By
Tempera on panel. 17 1/2 x 27 inches.
Signed lower right: *Andrew Wyeth*. Painted in 1949–1950.
Despite the apparent photographic realism of the painting, Wyeth has concentrated the elements in a highly controlled and carefully composed manner. The arid technique and muted palette skillfully support his customary theme of loneliness, here an unusually dramatic handling of superstitious anxiety.

Collection:
The Metropolitan Museum of Art, New York. Arthur H. Hearn Fund, 1950.
Exhibition:
Washington, D.C., Corcoran Gallery, *The American Muse*, 1959, no. 95.
Bibliography:
H. Geldzahler, *American Paintings in the 20th Century*, New York, 1965, pp. 175–176, repr. p. 176.

89 DICKINSON. Ruin at Daphne
90 WYETH. A Crow Flew By

LARRY RIVERS (born 1923)

Born in New York, Rivers studied at the Juilliard School of Music in New York in 1944 and 1945, was a jazz musician for two years, then studied painting with Hans Hofmann and at N.Y.U. in 1947 and 1948. Most closely associated with the Abstract Expressionists of the fifties, he has applied the vitality and scale of their technique to figurative art. Within that framework, his painting assimilates various elements of imagery – labels, signs, references to old master paintings – usually associated with the Pop artists of the sixties.

91
The Sitter

Oil on canvas. 51 1/8 x 47 inches.
Painted in 1956.

Rivers' considerable skill as a draftsman is apparent, but of greater interest is his seemingly impulsive manipulation of relationships within the highly flexible space of the painting. The same objects seem to be viewed from more than one point or reappear in different contexts. The sense of fluidity and movement is felt too in the Expressionist brevity of handling.

Collection:
The Metropolitan Museum of Art, New York. Gift of Hugo Kastor, 1956.
Exhibition:
New York, Metropolitan Museum, *Three Centuries of American Painting*, 1965.
Bibliography:
H. Geldzahler, *American Painting in the 20th Century*, New York, 1965, pp. 174–175, repr. p. 174.

LEE GATCH (1902–1968)

Gatch, who was born in Baltimore, studied with Leon Kroll and John Sloan at the Maryland Institute of Fine Arts from 1920 to 1924. Then, in the space of a year, he entered the American School in Fontainebleau, France, and after travels in France and Italy, worked with André Lhote and Moïse Kisling at the Académie Moderne in Paris. During the next decade Gatch worked in New York developing a lyric form of semi-abstraction. In 1935, he moved to his permanent home in Lambertville, N.J., where his style, founded on Cubism, became totally abstract in the last years of his life.

92
Night Gothic

Oil on canvas. 42 1/4 x 46 1/4 inches.
Signed lower left: *L Gatch*. Painted in 1957.

Gatch's paintings of the forties and fifties are subtly and romantically conceived compositions of forms from nature, simplified and patterned in a Cubist manner. His colors are softly and delicately applied, almost stained into the canvas. His sensitive and decorative designs of planar forms, similar to the work of Milton Avery, have sustained at a high level the romantic tradition of American landscape.

Collection:
Museum of Fine Arts, Boston. Charles Henry Hayden Fund, 1957.
Exhibition:
American Federation of Arts, New York, circulated in the U.S., *Gatch Retrospective*, 1960–1961, pp. 12, 19–20, no. 37, repr.
Bibliography:
B. Guest, "Avery and Gatch," *Art News*, March, 1960, p. 44.

STUART DAVIS (1894–1964)

Born in Philadelphia, Davis sought out Robert Henri in New York in 1910. Extremely talented, his work was included in the Armory Show three years later. Revelations there disenchanted him with Ashcan School realism. He first experimented with a colorful expressionism inspired by Van Gogh and Gauguin, but in a few years was painting Cubist abstractions, the primary course of his career. In the twenties and thirties he introduced commercial labels and similar figurative elements into his highly decorative two-dimensional designs. His forceful colors and complex angular compositions developed pulsating rhythms reflecting the frantic action of city life. As one of the earliest and finest of American abstractionists, Davis' art, writing and teaching had an important effect on the new generation of abstractionists that developed in New York in the later 1940's.

93
Semé

Oil on canvas. 52 x 40 inches.
Signed upper right: *Stuart Davis*. Painted in 1953.

The dynamism of Davis' vibrant colors and staccato rhythms of overlapping, jagged shapes create an optical excitement unique in modern American painting. His injection of words, numbers and letters into his works temporarily arrest the eye and also form part of the overall composition. The artist interprets the title as "strewn," many things brought together.

Collection:
The Metropolitan Museum of Art, New York. George A. Hearn Fund, 1953.
Exhibition:
New York, Metropolitan Museum, *Three Centuries of American Painting*, 1965.
Bibliography:
H. Geldzahler, *American Painting in the 20th Century*, New York, 1965, p. 146, repr. p. 147.

91 RIVERS. The Sitter

92 GATCH. Night Gothic

93 DAVIS. Semé

94 HOFMANN. Art – Like Love is Dedication

95   DE KOONING. Easter Monday

HANS HOFMANN (1880–1966)

German by birth, before emigrating to America in 1932, Hofmann had already been extremely active in the germinal art movements of Germany and France. First exposed to Impressionism in Munich, he then met Picasso, Braque and Matisse in Paris, and became a close friend of Delaunay. His work developed in the Cubist manner and in 1914, he opened an extremely successful art school. On moving to America, Hofmann taught at the University of California, then settled in New York and Provincetown, where he established important art schools. Through his personal dynamism and intentive solutions for composition through color, he became a brilliant and influential teacher.

94
Art – Like Love is Dedication

Oil on canvas. 60 x 52 inches.
Signed and dated lower right: *hans hofmann 65.*
The free application and interplay of saturated color planes, some thinly washed and others densely piled on top, is only one of several stylistic variations used by Hofmann during the last decade of his life. The explosive vitality is reminiscent of Abstract Expressionism, but he consciously structures space through color itself in a powerful and personal way.

Collection:
Mrs. Susan Morse Hilles, New Haven, Conn.
Museum of Fine Arts, Boston. Intended Gift of Susan Morse Hilles.
Exhibition:
Boston, MFA, *Centennial Acquisitions: Art Treasures for Tomorrow,* 1970, no. 119, repr. p. 158.

WILLEM DE KOONING (born 1904)

Born in Rotterdam, Holland, de Kooning emigrated to the United States in 1926. He soon met Gorky and others who, with himself, would figure importantly in the Abstract Expressionist movement of the forties and fifties. A figure and portrait painter until 1940, de Kooning then developed a partly Cubist abstract style, which remained essentially biomorphic in concern. By the fifties, his highly personal and broadly expressionist style alternated between the figural and the abstract. De Kooning's dynamic, violent and vividly colored series devoted to women formed a peak of achievement. His impact on Kline, Tworkov and others was also of great significance for the direction of Abstract Expressionist painting.

95
Easter Monday

Oil and newspaper transfer on canvas. 96 x 74 inches.
Signed lower left: *de Kooning.* Painted in 1955–1956.
The slashing brushwork characterizes the artist's intense and immediate involvement – stimulating an empathetic response in the viewer – in the work and the act of its creation. De Kooning's painting retains, despite its energy of execution, a persistent concern for formal shapes.

Collection:
The Metropolitan Museum of Art, New York. Rogers Fund, 1956.
Exhibitions:
New York, Museum of Modern Art, *De Kooning,* 1968–1969, no. 72, repr. p. 109; New York, Metropolitan Museum, *New York Painting and Sculpture: 1940–1970,* 1969–1970, no. 64, repr. p. 139.
Bibliography:
H. Geldzahler, *American Painting in the 20th Century,* New York, 1965, p. 197, repr. p. 198.

FRANZ KLINE (1910–1962)

Although Kline is known almost exclusively for his dramatic Abstract Expressionist paintings, they occupied only the last dozen years of his career. Born in Wilkes-Barre, Pa., he studied in Philadelphia, at the Art School of Boston University from 1931 to 1935, and for a year in London. Through the 1940's, his work was essentially realistic, with roots in the art of the Ashcan School. Compelled by the gestural dynamism of the painting of Jackson Pollock and Willem de Kooning, about 1949 Kline abandoned his realistic painting of urban genre for large scale, bold abstractions violently painted in contrasting black and white. During the succeeding years, he became one of the foremost Abstract Expressionist artists.

96
Probst I

Oil on canvas. 108 x 79$\frac{5}{8}$ inches.
Signed and dated on back center: *Franz Kline –60.*
Painted only two years before the artist's death, the scale, complexity and addition of color anticipate new stylistic developments. Its jagged structural shapes are possibly reminiscent of the forms of the city itself.

Collection:
Mrs. Susan Morse Hilles, New Haven, Conn., 1962.
Museum of Fine Arts, Boston. Promised gift of Susan Morse Hilles.
Exhibitions:
New York, Whitney Museum, *Kline,* 1968, no. 77; Boston, MFA, *Centennial Acquisitions: Art Treasures for Tomorrow,* 1970, no. 120, repr. p. 159.

96 KLINE. Probst I

97 GOTTLIEB. Thrust

ADOLPH GOTTLIEB (born 1903)

Gottlieb, born in New York City, studied at the Arts Students League under John Sloan and Robert Henri. Trips to Europe in the thirties did not importantly affect his work, but like Rothko and others he did feel the effect of the numbers of artists who left Europe in that decade, the Surrealists in particular. The Pictographs of the forties and the Burst series begun in 1957 are the two major periods of his art, and both fall within the Abstract Expressionist aesthetic. Strong color and an intense immediacy are characteristic of both periods. Gottlieb utilized a vocabulary of intuitive primitivism in the former and explosive gesture in the latter.

97
Thrust

Oil on canvas. 108 x 90 inches.
Signed and dated on the back: *Adolph Gottlieb* / 1959.
In the Bursts, Gottlieb reduces the complex symbolism of the Pictographs to but a few. *Thrust* contains only two, one coolly geometric, the other brutally explosive. Both hover in a broad field of color which absorbs the viewer into its world. In the series, the polarity of shapes and colors is essentially constant; it is the specific color choices which contain the significance of the individual work.

Collection:
The Metropolitan Museum of Art, New York. George A. Hearn Fund, 1959.
Exhibition:
New York, Metropolitan Museum, *New York Painting and Sculpture: 1940–1970*, 1969–1970, no. 102, p. 166, repr.
Bibliography:
H. Geldzahler, *American Painting in the 20th Century*, New York, 1965, p. 190, repr. p. 191.

ROBERT MOTHERWELL (born 1915)

While born in Aberdeen, Wash., and raised in San Francisco, New York is Motherwell's true home. Articulate and intellectually oriented, he was first trained in art history, criticism and philosophy, and as a painter is largely self-taught. Acquaintance with European Surrealists in the early 1940's interested him in automatism – an intuitive approach to painting. He then met several of the Abstract Expressionists and worked with Pollock and Rothko, developing a powerfully structured form of abstraction by the late 1940's. Fruition of this development came with the commanding series of more than 100 works called *Elegies to the Spanish Republic*. More recently, and perhaps an outgrowth of his earlier concepts is the radically minimal "Open" series.

98
Elegy to the Spanish Republic, 70

Oil on canvas. 69 x 114 inches.
Painted in 1961.
Motherwell is best known for the *Spanish Elegies*, a series begun in 1949 which continued through most of the sixties. They are primarily large scale compositions, aggressively painted rectangular and ovoid structures in black and white, occasionally with ochre. Not specifically political, they are monumental personal metaphors on both the fall of the Spanish Republic and the more essential concepts of life and death.

Collection:
The Metropolitan Museum of Art, New York. Anonymous Gift, 1965.
Exhibitions:
New York, Guggenheim Museum, and circulated in Europe and North and South

98 MOTHERWELL. Elegy to the Spanish Republic, 70

America, *Guggenheim International Award*, 1964, pp. 13, 31, 60, no. 78, repr.; New York, Metropolitan Museum, *New York Painting and Sculpture: 1940–1970*, 1969–1970, no. 256, repr. p. 233.

Bibliography:

H. H. Arnason, "Robert Motherwell: The Years 1948 to 1965," *Art International*, April, 1966, p. 30.

ELLSWORTH KELLY (born 1923)

Kelly, born in Newburgh, N. Y., was a leader during the 1950's of the New York hard-edge abstract painters who sought controlled, usually geometric alternatives to the intuitive, gestural styles of the Abstract Expressionists. Both the simplified color areas of his painting and the sensitive outlines of his drawings of plants and flowers relate in part to the art of Matisse. The strength of his work lies in the sophisticated balance of colors and shapes which at one time can appear to touch or overlap. In more recent years, he has worked with the shaped canvas, and sculpture, in which a few flatly painted areas enforce the shape of the object.

99
Blue Red Green

Oil on canvas. 91 x 82 inches.
Painted in 1962–1963.

In the fifties and sixties a wide variety of types of formal abstraction developed, as did equally varied terms for identification: post-painterly abstraction, systemic art, minimal, hard-edge and color field painting. Among the different approaches, ranging from Olitski, Louis and Frankenthaler to Stella, Held and Noland, Kelly's painting is distinct for its controlled interplay of a very few basic shapes and colors.

Collection:

The Metropolitan Museum of Art, New York. Arthur H. Hearn Fund, 1963.

Exhibition:

New York, Metropolitan Museum, *New York Painting and Sculpture: 1940–1970*, 1969–1970, no. 175, repr. p. 200.

Bibliography:

H. Geldzahler, *American Painting in the 20th Century*, New York, 1965, pp. 151–152, repr. p. 151.

HELEN FRANKENTHALER (born 1928)

Helen Frankenthaler, the wife of Robert Motherwell, was born in New York City. She has studied with Rufino Tamayo, at Bennington College with Paul Feeley, and with Hans Hofmann among others. Her perception in 1951 of the significance of Jackson Pollock's work led to her creation of a new form of painting that radically changed the direction and development of abstract art. By staining fresh, bright colors directly into raw canvas she established a unified compositional surface, unrelated to a specific orientation and breaking with traditional concepts of space. These free forms and open organization, combined with the staining technique have provided a bridge between the Abstract Expressionists and color-field painters. The visit of Morris Louis and Kenneth Noland to her studio in 1953 inspired Louis to begin his sensitive, transparently colored *Veils* of 1954 through 1958. The painting of Kenneth Noland and Jules Olitski also relate directly to her work.

100
Stride

Acrylic on canvas. 117 x 94 inches.
Painted in 1969.

The absence of paint texture, making the color shape a part of the canvas, permits the composition to hover in an undefined space. While the design in some of the more recent works, vast in size and scale, appears to relate to the edges of the canvas, truncation of shapes by the edge implies a potentially limitless picture world.

Collection:

The Metropolitan Museum of Art, New York. Anonymous Gift, 1970.

Exhibition:

New York, André Emmerich Gallery, *Helen Frankenthaler New Paintings*, 1969.

99 KELLY. Blue Red Green

100 FRANKENTHALER. Stride

Bibliography

SOURCE WORKS

Dictionary of American Biography, edited by Allen Johnson and Dumas Malone, 20 vols., New York, 1928–1936.

Mantle Fielding. *Dictionary of American Painters, Sculptors and Engravers*, Philadelphia, 1926.

Albert T. E. Gardner and Stuart P. Feld. *American Paintings, a Catalogue of the Collection of The Metropolitan Museum of Art. I. Painters Born by 1815*, New York, 1965.

George C. Groce and David H. Wallace. *The New-York Historical Society's Dictionary of Artists in America, 1564–1860*, New Haven and London, 1957.

Leo Lerman. *The Museum One Hundred Years and The Metropolitan Museum of Art*, introduction by Thomas P. F. Hoving, New York, 1969.

Museum of Fine Arts, Boston. *M. and M. Karolik Collection of American Paintings 1815 to 1865*, Cambridge, Massachusetts, 1949.

—. *M. and M. Karolik Collection of American Water Colors and Drawings*, 2 vols., Boston, 1962.

Walter Muir Whitehall, *Museum of Fine Arts, Boston, A Centennial History*, 2 vols., Cambridge, Mass., 1970.

GENERAL WORKS

Lawrence Alloway. "The New American Painting", in *Art International*, III, nos. 3–4, 1959.

Dore Ashton. *The Unknown Shore: A View of Contemporary Art*, Boston, 1962.

Virgil Barker. *American Painting, History and Interpretation*, New York, 1950.

Alfred H. Barr, Jr. *Cubism and Abstract Art*, New York, 1936.

George Battock, ed. *Minimal Art*, New York, 1968.

—. *The New Art*, New York, 1966.

John I. H. Baur. *Revolution and Tradition in Modern American Art*, Cambridge, Massachusetts, 1961.

Mary Black and Jean Lipman. *American Folk Painting*, New York, 1966.

Rudi Blesh. *Modern Art USA*, New York, 1956.

Wolfgang Born. *American Landscape Painting, an Interpretation*, New Haven, 1948.

—. *Still-Life Painting in America*, New York, 1947.

Milton Brown. *American Painting from the Armory Show to the Depression*, Princeton, 1955.

Alan Burroughs. *Limners and Likenesses, Three Centuries of American Painting*, Cambridge, Massachusetts, 1936.

Holger Cahill and Alfred H. Barr, Jr. *Art in America: A Complete Survey*, New York, 1934.

James T. Callow. *Kindred Spirits, Knickerbocker Writers and American Artists, 1807–1855*, Chapel Hill, North Carolina, 1967.

Royal Cortissoz. *American Artists*, New York and London, 1923.

William Dunlap. *History of the Rise and Progress of the Arts of Design in the United States*, introduction by William Campbell, edited by Alexander Wyckoff, 3 vols., New York, 1965.

Alexander Eliot. *Three Hundred Years of American Painting*, New York, 1957.

James T. Flexner. *America's Old Masters; First Artists of the New World*, New York, 1939.

—. *American Painting: The Light of Distant Skies, 1760–1835*, New York, 1954.

—. *First Flowers of Our Wilderness*, Boston, 1947.

—. *That Wilder Image, the Painting of America's Native School from Thomas Cole to Winslow Homer*, Boston and Toronto, 1962.

Alfred Frankenstein. *After the Hunt: William Harnett and Other American Still-Life Painters, 1870–1900*, revised edition, California Studies in the History of Art, vol. 12, Berkeley and Los Angeles, 1969.

Henry Geldzahler. *American Painting in the 20th Century*, New York, 1965.

Clement Greenberg. *Art and Culture*, Boston, 1961.

Horatio Greenough. *The Travels, Observations and Experiences of a Yankee Stonecutter*, New York, 1852.

Thomas B. Hess. *Abstract Painting: Background and American Phase*, New York, 1951.

Samuel Isham. *A History of American Painting*, New York, 1905; reprinted with additions by Royal Cortissoz, New York, 1927.

Oliver W. Larkin. *Art and Life in America*, New York, 1960.

Lucy R. Lippard. *Pop Art*, New York, 1966.

John W. McCourbey, ed. *American Art 1700–1960, Sources and Documents*, Englewood Cliffs, New Jersey, 1965.

—. *American Tradition in Painting*, New York, 1963.

Richard McLanathan. *The American Tradition in the Arts*, New York, 1968.

Robert Motherwell and Ad Reinhardt, eds. *Modern Artists in America*, New York, 1951.

Barbara Novak. *American Painting of the Nineteenth Century, Realism, Idealism, and the American Experience*, New York, 1969.

Jules David Prown and Barbara Rose. *American Painting*, 2 vols., Geneva, 1969.

Edgar P. Richardson. *American Romantic Painting*, New York, 1944.

—. *Painting in America: The Story of 450 Years*, New York, 1956.

Barbara Rose. *American Art Since 1900: A Critical History*, New York and Washington, 1967.

—. *Readings in American Art Since 1900*, New York, 1967.

Clara E. Sears. *Highlights Among the Hudson River Artists*, Boston, 1947.

James Thrall Soby and Dorothy Miller, *Romantic Painting in America*, New York, 1943.

Henry T. Tuckerman. *Artist-Life: Or Sketches of American Painters*, New York and Philadelphia, 1847.

Monroe Wheeler. *Painters and Sculptors of Modern America*, New York, 1942.

John Wilmerding. *A History of American Marine Painting*, Boston and Toronto, 1968.

GENERAL EXHIBITIONS

1909

The Metropolitan Museum of Art, New York, *The Hudson-Fulton Celebration*.

1911

The Metropolitan Museum of Art, New York, *Colonial Portraits*.

1933

The Art Insitute of Chicago, *Century of Progress*.

1934

Worcester Art Museum, Worcester, Massachusetts, *XVIIth Century Painting in New England*, catalogue by Louisa Dresser.

1937

Brooklyn Museum, *Leaders of American Impressionism, Mary Cassatt, Childe Hassam, John H. Twachtman, J. Alden Weir*, introduction by John I. H. Baur.

1938

Musée du Jeu de Paume, Paris, *Trois Siècles d'Art aux Etats-Unis*.

1939

The Metropolitan Museum of Art, New York, *Life in America*.
Museum of Modern Art, New York, *Art in Our Time*.
New York, World's Fair, *Masterpieces of Art*.

1940

The Baltimore Museum of Art, *Romanticism in America*.

1943

Museum of Modern Art, New York, *American Realists and Magic Realists*, catalogue by Dorothy Miller and Alfred H. Barr, Jr.
Museum of Modern Art, New York, *Romantic Painting in America*.

1945

The Art Institute of Chicago and Whitney Museum of American Art, New York, *The Hudson River School and the Early American Landscape Tradition*, catalogue by Frederick A. Sweet.

1946

Tate Gallery, London, *American Painting*.

1951

The Detroit Institute of Arts and The Toledo Museum of Art, *Travelers in Arcadia, American Artists in Italy, 1830–1875*, catalogue by Edgar P. Richardson and Otto Wittman, Jr.
National Academy of Design, New York, *The American Tradition*.

1953

The American Federation of Arts, New York, *American Painting in the Nineteenth Century* (circulated to the Whitney Museum of American Art, New York, and in Germany and Italy).

1954

The Art Institute of Chicago and The Metropolitan Museum of Art, New York, *Sargent, Whistler and Mary Cassatt*, catalogue by Frederick A. Sweet.

1957

Brooklyn Museum, *Face of America*.

1959

The Baltimore Museum of Art, *The Age of Elegance: Rococo and Its Effect*.
The Corcoran Gallery of Art, Washington, D.C., *The American Muse*.

1960

Walker Art Center, Minneapolis, *The Precisionist View of American Art* (circulated in the U.S.).

1961

The Metropolitan Museum of Art, New York, *101 Masterpieces of American Primitive Painting from the Collection of Edgar William and Bernice Chrysler Garbisch* (circulated by The American Federation of Arts, New York, 1962–1964).
The Solomon R. Guggenheim Museum, New York, *American Abstract Expressionists and Imagists*, catalogue by H. H. Arnason.

1963

The Jewish Museum, New York, *Toward a New Abstraction*.

1964

Marlborough-Gerson Gallery, New York, *Jackson Pollock*, catalogue by Sam Hunter.
Museum of Modern Art, New York, *The Responsive Eye*, catalogue by William C. Seitz.
New York, World's Fair, *Four Centuries of American Masterpieces*.

1965

Fogg Art Museum, Cambridge, Massachu-

setts, *Three American Painters* (Olitski, Noland, Stella), catalogue by Michael Fried.
Los Angeles County Museum of Art, *The New York School: The First Generation.*
The Metropolitan Museum of Art, New York, *Three Centuries of American Painting.*

1966
Museum of Modern Art, New York, *Two Decades of American Painting* (circulated to Japan, India, and Australia).
The Solomon R. Guggenheim Museum, New York, *Systemic Painting*, catalogue by Lawrence Alloway.

1967
Brooklyn Museum, Virginia Museum of Fine Arts, Richmond, and California Palace of the Legion of Honor, San Francisco, *Triumph of Realism; an Exhibition of European and American Realist Paintings 1850–1910.*

1969
The Metropolitan Museum of Art, New York, *New York Painting and Sculpture: 1940–1970*, catalogue by Henry Geldzahler.

1970
The Metropolitan Museum of Art, New York, *Masterpieces of Painting in The Metropolitan Museum of Art*, exhibited at the Museum of Fine Arts, Boston.
The Metropolitan Museum of Art, New York, *19th-Century America: Paintings and Sculpture.*
Museum of Fine Arts, Boston, *Centennial Acquisitions: Art Treasures for Tomorrow.*
Museum of Fine Arts, Boston, *100 Paintings from the Boston Museum*, exhibited at The Metropolitan Museum of Art, New York.

INDIVIDUAL ARTISTS
Selected Publications and Exhibitions

WASHINGTON ALLSTON
Jared B. Flagg. *The Life and Letters of Washington Allston*, New York, 1892.

Edgar P. Richardson. *Washington Allston: A Study of the Romantic Artist in America*, Chicago, 1948.

The Detroit Institute of Arts and Museum of Fine Arts, Boston. *Washington Allston 1779–1843, a Loan Exhibition of Paintings, Drawings and Memorabilia*, catalogue by Edgar P. Richardson, 1947.

MILTON AVERY
Barbara Guest. "Avery and Gatch," *Art News*, March, 1960.

Hilton Kramer. *Milton Avery: Paintings 1930–1960*, New York, 1962.

Sheldon Memorial Art Gallery, Lincoln, Nebraska, and Arkansas Art Center, Little Rock. *Milton Avery*, 1966.

JOSEPH BADGER
Lawrence Park. "An Account of the Work of Joseph Badger, and a Descriptive List of His Work," *Proceedings of the Massachusetts Historical Society*, LI, December, 1917.

GEORGE BELLOWS
Emma S. Bellows. *Paintings of Bellows*, New York, 1929.

Charles H. Morgan. *George Bellows*, New York, 1965.

The Art Institute of Chicago. *George Bellows, Paintings, Drawings and Prints*, 1946.

ALBERT BIERSTADT
Gordon Hendricks. "The First Three Western Journeys of Albert Bierstadt," *The Art Bulletin*, September, 1964.

Santa Barbara Museum of Art. *A Retrospective Exhibition, Albert Bierstadt 1830–1902*, introduction by Thomas W. Leavitt, 1964.

GEORGE CALEB BINGHAM
E. Maurice Bloch. *George Caleb Bingham*, 2 vols., California Studies in the History of Art, vol. 7, Berkeley and Los Angeles, 1967.

Albert Christ-Janer. *George Caleb Bingham of Missouri*, New York, 1940.

John Francis McDermott. *George Caleb Bingham, River Portraitist*, Norman, Oklahoma, 1959.

National Collection of Fine Arts, Washington, D.C., The Cleveland Museum of Art, and the Art Galleries, University of California at Los Angeles. *George Caleb Bingham 1811–1879*, introduction by E. Maurice Bloch, 1967.

JOSEPH BLACKBURN
Lawrence Park. *Joseph Blackburn, Colonial Portrait Painter, with a Descriptive List of His Works*, Worcester, Massachusetts, 1923.

John Hill Morgan and Henry Wilder Foote. *An Extension of Lawrence Park's Descriptive List of the Work of Joseph Blackburn*, Worcester, Massachusetts, 1937.

RALPH ALBERT BLAKELOCK
Elliott Daingerfield. *Ralph Albert Blakelock*, New York, 1914.

Whitney Museum of American Art, New York. *Ralph Albert Blakelock Centenary Exhibition in Celebration of the Centennial of the City College of New York*, introduction by Lloyd Goodrich, 1947.

The Art Galleries, University of California, Santa Barbara, California Palace of the Legion of Honor, San Francisco, Phoenix Art Museum, and The Heckscher Museum, Huntington, New York. *The Enigma of Ralph A. Blakelock 1847–1919*, catalogue by David Gebhard and Phyllis Stuurman, 1969.

MARY CASSATT
Adelyn D. Breeskin. *The Graphic Work of Mary Cassatt, a Catalogue Raisonné*, New York, 1948.

Barbara N. Parker. "A Philadelphian in Paris," Museum of Fine Arts, Boston, *Bulletin*, 1942, XL, no. 240.

Frederick A. Sweet. *Miss Mary Cassatt, Impressionist from Pennsylvania*, Norman, Oklahoma, 1966.

Forbes Watson. *Mary Cassatt*, American Artists Series, New York, 1932.

The Baltimore Museum of Art. *Mary Cassatt. The Catalogue of a Comprehensive Exhibition of Her Work*, 1941.

The Baltimore Museum of Art. *Manet, Degas, Cassatt, Morisot*, 1962.

FREDERIC EDWIN CHURCH

David C. Huntington. *The Landscapes of Frederic Edwin Church: Vision of an American Era*, New York, 1966.

National Collection of Fine Arts, Washington, D.C., Albany Institute of History and Art, Albany, New York, and M. Knoedler and Company, New York. *Frederic Edwin Church*, introduction by David C. Huntington, 1966.

THOMAS COLE

The Baltimore Museum of Art. *Annual II. Studies on Thomas Cole, an American Romanticist*, 1967.

Elliott S. Vesell. *The Life and Works of Thomas Cole*, Cambridge, Massachusetts, 1964.

Wadsworth Atheneum, Hartford, and Whitney Museum of American Art, New York. *Thomas Cole 1801–1848, One Hundred Years Later*, catalogue by Esther Isabel Seaver, 1948.

Rochester Memorial Art Gallery of the University of Rochester, Rochester, New York, Munson-Williams-Proctor Institute, Utica, New York, Albany Institute of History and Art, Albany, New York, and Whitney Museum of American Art, New York. *Thomas Cole*, catalogue by Howard S. Merritt, 1969.

JOHN SINGLETON COPLEY

Barbara N. Parker and Anne B. Wheeler. *John Singleton Copley*, Boston, 1938.

Augustus T. Perkins. *A Sketch of the Life and a List of Some Works of John Singleton Copley*, Boston, 1873.

Jules David Prown. *John Singleton Copley*, 2 vols., Cambridge, Massachusetts, 1966.

Edgar P. Richardson. "Watson and the Shark by Copley," *Art Quarterly*, 1947, X, no. 3.

National Gallery of Art, Washington, D.C., The Metropolitan Museum of Art, New York, and Museum of Fine Arts, Boston, *John Singleton Copley*, catalogue by Jules David Prown, 1965–1966.

JASPER FRANCIS CROPSEY

University of Maryland Art Gallery, College Park. *Jasper F. Cropsey 1823–1900, a Retrospective View of America's Painter of Autumn*, catalogue by Peter Bermingham, preface by George Levitine, foreword by William H. Gerdts, 1968.

STUART DAVIS

Eugene C. Goossen. *Stuart Davis*, New York, 1959.

National Collection of Fine Arts, Washington, D.C. *Stuart Davis Memorial Exhibition*, catalogue by H. H. Arnason, 1965.

WILLEM DE KOONING

Thomas B. Hess. *Willem De Kooning*, New York, 1959.

Museum of Modern Art, New York. *Willem De Kooning*, catalogue by Thomas B. Hess, 1968.

EDWIN DICKINSON

Elaine De Kooning. "Edwin Dickinson Paints a Picture," *Art News*, September, 1949.

Whitney Museum of American Art, New York. *Edwin Dickinson*, catalogue by Lloyd Goodrich, 1965.

ASHER BROWN DURAND

John Durand. *The Life and Times of Asher B Durand*, New York, 1894.

THOMAS COWPERTHWAIT EAKINS

C. C. Cunningham. "A Sporting Picture by Eakins," Museum of Fine Arts, Boston, *Bulletin*, 1936, XXXIV, no. 201.

Lloyd Goodrich. *Thomas Eakins. His Life and Work*, New York, 1933.

National Gallery of Art, Washington, D.C., The Art Institute of Chicago, and Philadelphia Museum of Art. *Thomas Eakins, a Retrospective Exhibition*, introduction by Lloyd Goodrich, 1961–1962.

Whitney Museum of American Art, New York. *Eakins,* catalogue by Lloyd Goodrich, 1970.

RALPH EARL

Laurence B. Goodrich. *Ralph Earl: Recorder for an Era*, Albany, New York, 1967.

William Sawitzky. *Ralph Earl, 1751–1801*, New York and Worcester, Massachusetts, 1945.

LYONEL FEININGER

Hans Hess. *Feininger*. New York, 1961.

Museum of Modern Art, New York. *Lyonel Feininger, Marsden Hartley* edited by Dorothy C. Miller, New York, 1944.

The Cleveland Museum of Art (and circulated in the U.S.). *Feininger Memorial*, 1959–1961.

The Pasadena Art Museum, Milwaukee Art Center, and The Baltimore Museum of Art. *Lyonel Feininger, 1871–1956; a Memorial Exhibition*, 1966.

ROBERT FEKE

Henry Wilder Foote. *Robert Feke, Colonial Portrait Painter*, Cambridge, Massachusetts, 1930.

Barbara N. Parker. "A Member of the Winslow Family in Boston," Museum of Fine Arts, Boston, *Bulletin*, 1942, XL, no. 241.

Whitney Museum of American Art, New York, The Heckscher Museum, Huntington, New York, and Museum of Fine Arts, Boston. *Robert Feke*, 1946.

ERASTUS SALISBURY FIELD

Thomas N. Maytham. "Two Faces of New England Portrait Painting," Museum of Fine Arts, Boston, *Bulletin*, 1963, LXI, no. 323.

Abby Aldrich Rockefeller Folk Art Collection, Williamsburg, Virginia. *Field,* 1963.

HELEN FRANKENTHALER

Barbara Rose. "Painting Within the Tradition, the Career of Helen Frankenthaler," *Artforum*, April, 1969.

Whitney Museum of American Art, New York (and circulated in Europe). *Helen Frankenthaler*, catalogue by E. C. Goossen, 1969.

LEE GATCH

Barbara Guest. "Avery and Gatch," *Art News*, March, 1960.

The American Federation of Arts, New York (circulated in the U. S.). *Lee Gatch,* catalogue by Perry T. Rathbone, 1960–1961.

SANFORD ROBINSON GIFFORD

James T. Flexner. *That Wilder Image, the Painting of America's Native School from Thomas Cole to Winslow Homer,* Boston and Toronto, 1962.

ADOLPH GOTTLIEB

Walker Art Center, Minneapolis. *Adolph Gottlieb,* catalogue by Martin Friedman, 1963.

Whitney Museum of American Art and The Solomon R. Guggenheim Museum, New York. *Adolph Gottlieb,* catalogue by Robert Doty and Diane Waldman, 1968.

CHESTER HARDING

Chester Harding. *My Egotistography,* Cambridge, Massachusetts, 1866. Reprinted as *A Sketch of Chester Harding, Artist, Drawn by His Own Hand,* edited and with preface by Margaret E. White, Boston and New York, 1890. Reprinted and annotated by W. P. G. Harding, Boston and New York, 1929.

WILLIAM MICHAEL HARNETT

Alfred Frankenstein. *After the Hunt: William Harnett and Other American Still-Life Painters, 1870–1900,* revised edition, California Studies in the History of Art, vol. 12, Berkeley and Los Angeles, 1969.

California Palace of the Legion of Honor, San Francisco. *Illusionism and Trompe l'Œil,* 1949.

La Jolla Museum of Art and Santa Barbara Museum of Art. *The Reminiscent Object, Paintings by William Michael Harnett, John Frederick Peto and John Haberle,* introduction by Alfred Frankenstein, 1965.

MARSDEN HARTLEY

Elizabeth McCausland. *Marsden Hartley,* Minneapolis, 1952.

Museum of Modern Art, New York. *Lyonel Feininger, Marsden Hartley* (essays), edited by Dorothy C. Miller, New York, 1944.

FREDERICK CHILDE HASSAM

Adeline Adams. *Childe Hassam,* New York, 1938.

The Corcoran Gallery of Art, Washington, D. C., Museum of Fine Arts, Boston, The Currier Gallery of Art, Manchester, New Hampshire, and Gallery of Modern Art, New York. *Childe Hassam, a Retrospective Exhibition,* foreword by Hermann Warner Williams, Jr., introduction by Charles E. Buckley, Jr., 1965.

RUFUS HATHAWAY

Nina F. Little. "Doctor Rufus Hathaway, Physician and Painter of Duxbury, Mass., 1770–1822". *Art in America,* 1953, XLI, no. 3.

MARTIN JOHNSON HEADE

Robert George McIntyre. *Martin Johnson Heade, 1819–1904,* New York, 1948.

Museum of Fine Arts, Boston, University of Maryland Art Gallery, College Park, and Whitney Museum of American Art, New York. *Martin Johnson Heade,* catalogue by Theodore E. Stebbins, Jr., 1969.

GEORGE PETER ALEXANDER HEALY

Marie De Mare. *G. P. A. Healy, American Artist, an Intimate Chronicle of the Nineteenth Century,* New York, 1954.

George P. A. Healy. *Reminiscences of a Portrait Painter,* Chicago, 1894.

ROBERT HENRI

Robert Henri. *The Art Spirit,* New York, 1923; new edition by Margery A. Ryerson, Philadelphia and New York, 1960.

Helen Appleton Read. *Robert Henri,* New York, 1931.

EDWARD HICKS

Alice E. Ford. *Edward Hicks, Painter of the Peaceable Kingdom,* Philadelphia, 1952.

HANS HOFMANN

Erle Loran. *Hans Hofmann,* Berkeley, California, 1964.

Museum of Modern Art, New York. *Hans Hofmann,* catalogue by William C. Seitz, 1963.

WINSLOW HOMER

Philip C. Beam. *Winslow Homer at Prout's Neck,* Boston and Toronto, 1966.

James T. Flexner and the Editors of Time-Life Books, *The World of Winslow Homer, 1836–1910,* Time-Life Library of Art, New York, 1966.

Lloyd Goodrich. *Winslow Homer,* New York, 1944.

—. *Winslow Homer,* The Great American Artists Series, New York, 1959.

Whitney Museum of American Art, New York. *Homer Centenary,* 1936.

National Gallery of Art, Washington, D. C., and The Metropolitan Museum of Art, New York. *Winslow Homer,* introduction by Albert T. E. Gardner, 1958–1959.

Museum of Fine Arts, Boston. *Winslow Homer,* 1959.

Bowdoin College Museum of Art, Brunswick, Maine. *Homer at Prout's Neck,* 1966.

Museum of Graphic Art, New York, and participating museums. *The Graphic Art of Winslow Homer,* catalogue by Lloyd Goodrich, foreword by Donald H. Karshan, 1968–1970.

EDWARD HOPPER

Henry Geldzahler. "Edward Hopper," The Metropolitan Museum of Art, New York, *Bulletin,* November, 1962.

Whitney Museum of American Art, New York, The Art Institute of Chicago, and City Art Museum of St. Louis. *Edward Hopper,* catalogue by Lloyd Goodrich, 1964–1965.

National Collection of Fine Arts, Washington, D. C. (for the São Paolo Bienal, Brazil) and Brandeis University, Waltham, Massachusetts. *Edward Hopper,* 1967–1968.

WILLIAM MORRIS HUNT

Helen M. Knowlton. *Art-Life of William Morris Hunt,* London, 1899.

Martha A. S. Shannon. *Boston Days of William Morris Hunt,* Boston, 1923.

GEORGE INNESS

LeRoy Ireland. *The Works of George Inness, an Illustrated Catalogue Raisonné,* Austin, Texas, and London, 1965.

Elizabeth McCausland. *George Inness, an American Landscape Painter, 1825–1894,* New York, 1946.

University Art Museum of the University of Texas, Austin. *The Paintings of George Inness (1844–94)*, preface by LeRoy Ireland, introduction by Nicolai Cikovsky, Jr., notes by Donald B. Goodall, 1965–1966.

JOHN WESLEY JARVIS

Harold Edward Dickson. *John Wesley Jarvis, American Painter, 1780–1840*, New York, 1949.

EASTMAN JOHNSON

John I. H. Baur. *An American Genre Painter, Eastman Johnson, 1824–1906*, Brooklyn, New York, 1940.

Everett U. Crosby. *Eastman Johnson at Nantucket*, Nantucket, Massachusetts, 1944.

JOHN FREDERICK KENSETT

The American Federation of Arts, New York. *John Frederick Kensett, 1816–1872*, catalogue by John K. Howat, 1968.

FRANZ KLINE

Marlborough-Gerson Gallery, New York. *Franz Kline*, introduction by Robert Goldwater, 1967.

Whitney Museum of American Art, New York. *Franz Kline: 1910–1962*, catalogue by John Gordon, 1968.

FITZ HUGH LANE

John Wilmerding. *Fitz Hugh Lane, 1804–1865, American Marine Painter*, Salem, Massachusetts, 1964.

SAMUEL FINLEY BREESE MORSE

Oliver W. Larkin. *Samuel F. B. Morse and American Democratic Art*, New York, 1954.

The Metropolitan Museum of Art, New York. *Samuel F. B. Morse*, catalogue by Harry B. Wehle, 1932.

National Academy of Design, New York. *Morse Exhibition of Arts and Science . . .*, exhibited at The American Museum of Natural History, New York, 1950.

ROBERT MOTHERWELL

H. H. Arnason. "Robert Motherwell: The Years 1948 to 1965," *Art International*, April, 1966.

—. "Motherwell and the Window," *Art News*, Summer, 1969.

Museum of Modern Art, New York. *Robert Motherwell*, catalogue by Frank O'Hara, 1965.

WILLIAM SIDNEY MOUNT

Bartlett Cowdrey and Hermann W. Williams, Jr. *William Sidney Mount, 1807–1868: An American Painter*, New York, 1944.

Brooklyn Museum. *Mount*, 1942.

National Gallery of Art, Washington, D. C., City Art Museum of St. Louis, Whitney Museum of American Art, New York, and M. H. De Young Memorial Museum, San Francisco. *Painter of Rural America: William Sidney Mount 1807–1868*, catalogue by Alfred Frankenstein, introduction by Jane Des Grange, 1968–1969.

CHARLES WILLSON PEALE

Charles Coleman Sellers. *Charles Willson Peale*, 2 vols., Philadelphia, 1947.

—. "Portraits and Miniatures by Charles Willson Peale," *American Philosophical Society Transactions*, XLII, part I, Philadelphia, 1952.

Pennsylvania Academy of the Fine Arts, Philadelphia. *Catalogue of an Exhibition of Portraits by Charles Willson Peale, James Peale and Rembrandt Peale*, 1923.

Century Association, New York. *Paintings by Members of the Peale Family*, 1953.

The Detroit Institute of Arts and Munson-Williams-Proctor Institute, Utica, New York. *The Peale Family, Three Generations of American Artists*, edited by Charles H. Elam, articles by Charles Coleman Sellers, E. Grosvenor Paine, and Edward H. Dwight, 1967.

JOHN FREDERICK PETO

Alfred Frankenstein. *After the Hunt: William Harnett and Other American Still-Life Painters, 1870–1900*, revised edition, California Studies in the History of Art, vol. 12, Berkeley and Los Angeles, 1969.

Smith College Museum, Northampton, Massachusetts, Brooklyn Museum, and California Palace of the Legion of Honor, San Francisco. *John F. Peto*, catalogue by Alfred Frankenstein, 1950.

La Jolla Museum of Art and Santa Barbara Museum of Art. *The Reminiscent Object, Paintings by William Michael Harnett, John Frederick Peto and John Haberle*, introduction by Alfred Frankenstein, 1965.

MATTHEW PRATT

William Sawitzky. *Matthew Pratt, 1734–1805*, New York, 1942.

MAURICE BRAZIL PRENDERGAST

Museum of Fine Arts, Boston (circulated in the U. S.). *Maurice Prendergast*, catalogue by Hedley Howell Rhys, 1960–1961.

SEVERIN ROESEN

Wolfgang Born. *Still-Life Painting in America*, New York, 1947.

Alfred Frankenstein. *After the Hunt: William Harnett and Other American Still-Life Painters, 1870–1900*, revised edition, California Studies in the History of Art, vol. 12, Berkeley and Los Angeles, 1969.

ALBERT PINKHAM RYDER

Lloyd Goodrich. *Albert Pinkham Ryder*, The Great American Artists Series, New York, 1959.

Whitney Museum of American Art, New York, *Ryder*, 1947.

The Corcoran Gallery of Art, Washington, D. C., *Albert Pinkham Ryder*, introduction by Lloyd Goodrich, 1961.

HENRY SARGENT

Edgar P. Richardson. *American Romantic Painting*, New York, 1944.

JOHN SINGER SARGENT

Evan Charteris. *John Sargent*, New York, 1927.

William Howe Downes. *John S. Sargent: His Life and Work*, Boston, 1925.

David McKibbin. *Sargent's Boston with an Essay & a Biographical Summary & a Complete Checklist of Sargent's Portraits*, Boston, 1956.

Museum of Fine Arts, Boston. *Sargent Memorial*, 1925.

—. *Sargent's Boston*, 1956.

The Corcoran Gallery of Art, Washington,

D. C., The Cleveland Museum of Art, Worcester Art Museum, Worcester, Massachusetts, and Munson-Williams-Proctor Institute, Utica, New York. *The Private World of John Singer Sargent,* catalogue by Donelson F. Hoopes, foreword by Hermann W. Williams, Jr., 1964–1965.

CHARLES SHEELER

Constance Rourke. *Charles Sheeler: Artist in the American Tradition,* New York, 1938.

National Collection of Fine Arts, Washington, D. C., Philadelphia Museum of Art, and Whitney Museum of American Art, New York. *Charles Sheeler,* 1968–1969.

JOHN SLOAN

Van Wyck Brooks. *John Sloan, a Painter's Life,* New York, 1955.

John Sloan. *Gist of Art,* New York, 1939.

Whitney Museum of American Art, New York, The Corcoran Gallery of Art, Washington, D. C., and The Toledo Museum of Art. *John Sloan, 1871–1951,* 1952.

JOHN SMIBERT

Stuart P. Feld. "In the Latest London Manner," The Metropolitan Museum of Art, New York, *Bulletin,* May, 1963.

Henry Wilder Foote. *John Smibert,* Cambridge, Massachusetts, 1950.

John Smibert. *The Notebook of John Smibert,* edited by Sir David Evans, John Kerslake and Andrew Oliver, Boston, 1969.

Yale University Art Gallery, New Haven. *The Smibert Tradition,* 1949.

JOSEPH STELLA

Irma B. Jaffe. *Joseph Stella,* Cambridge, Massachusetts, 1970.

Whitney Museum of American Art, New York. *Joseph Stella,* catalogue by John I. H. Baur, 1963.

GILBERT STUART

John Hill Morgan and Mantle Fielding. *Life Portraits of Washington,* Philadelphia, 1931.

Lawrence Park. *Gilbert Stuart, an Illustrated Descriptive List of His Work,* 4 vols., New York, 1926.

John Herron Art Institute, Indianapolis. *Retrospective Exhibition of Portraits by Gilbert Stuart, 1755–1828,* 1942.

National Gallery of Art, Washington, D. C., and Museum of Art, Rhode Island School of Design, Providence. *Gilbert Stuart, Portraitist of the Young Republic, 1755–1828,* 1967.

THOMAS SULLY

Edward Biddle and Mantle Fielding. *The Life and Works of Thomas Sully, 1783–1872,* Philadelphia, 1921.

Charles H. Hart, ed. *A Register of Portraits Painted by Thomas Sully, 1801–1871,* Philadelphia, 1909.

Pennsylvania Academy of the Fine Arts, Philadelphia. *Catalogue of the Memorial Exhibition of Portraits by Thomas Sully,* 1922.

JEROME B. THOMPSON

B. N. Parker. "A 'Pic Nick,' Camden, Maine, by Jerome B. Thompson," Museum of Fine Arts, Boston, *Bulletin,* 1952, L, no. 282.

JOHN TRUMBULL

Theodore Sizer. *The Works of Colonel John Trumbull, Artist of the American Revolution,* New Haven and London, 1967.

John Trumbull. *The Autobiography of Colonel John Trumbull, Patriot, Artist, 1756–1843,* edited by Theodore Sizer, New Haven, 1953.
—. *Autobiography, Reminiscences and Letters of John Trumbull, from 1756–1841,* New York, 1841.

JOHN HENRY TWACHTMAN

Eliot Clark. *John Twachtman,* New York, 1924.

Cincinnati Art Museum. *A Retrospective Exhibition, John Henry Twachtman,* introduction by Richard J. Boyle, introduction to prints by Mary Welsh Baskett, 1966.

ELIHU VEDDER

Regina Soria. "Some Background Notes for Elihu Vedder's 'Cumean Sibyl' and 'Young Marsyas'," *Art Quarterly,* Spring, 1960.

Elihu Vedder. *The Digressions of V. Written for His Own Fun and That of His Friends,* Boston and New York, 1910.

BENJAMIN WEST

Grose Evans. *Benjamin West and the Taste of His Times,* Carbondale, Illinois, 1959.

John Galt. *Life, Studies, and Works of Benjamin West,* London, 1820.

JAMES ABBOTT McNEILL WHISTLER

Elizabeth R. Pennell and Joseph Pennell. *The Life of James McNeill Whistler,* 2 vols., London and Philadelphia, 1908.

Denys Sutton. *Nocturne: The Art of James McNeill Whistler,* Philadelphia and New York, 1964.
—. *James McNeill Whistler,* London, 1966.

The Arts Council Gallery, London, and M. Knoedler and Company, New York. *James McNeill Whistler, an Exhibition of Paintings and Other Works,* introduction by Andrew McLaren Young, 1960.

The Art Institute of Chicago and Munson-Williams-Proctor Institute, Utica, New York. *James McNeill Whistler,* catalogue by Frederick A. Sweet, 1968.

Index of Artists

Numbers refer to catalogue entry